Despite the growth of corporate power in our lives, most media outlets have failed to institutionalize regular, aggressive business reporting. Lewin and Reed offer a practical guide to establishing business journalism in large and small newsrooms.
Bill Barnhart, financial columnist, Chicago Tribune

Reed and Lewin offer hope for dysfunctional news operations everywhere with a management guide that's smart and practical and steeped with real-world examples. Nicely written too. Put it on the bookshelf between your Strunk and White and your 'Barron's Dictionary of Finance and Investment Terms.'
Glenn Coleman, assistant managing editor, Money

Bob and Glenn are as good at explaining the value of business writing as they are at helping reporters do a better job of it. I know a few editors who would do well to read this book.
William Spain, reporter, MarketWatch from Dow Jones

Reed and Lewin provide an actionable, thoughtful guide to the intricacies of the work of business news from the valuable perspective of people who have done that work successfully.
Bob Reichblum, former executive, CNBC and WebFN

Covering Business

A guide to aggressively reporting on commerce and developing a powerful business beat

Robert Reed and Glenn Lewin

Marion Street Press, Inc.
Oak Park, Illinois

ISBN 1-933338-01-6
Printed in U.S.A.
Printing 10 9 8 7 6 5 4 3 2 1

Marion Street Press, Inc.
PO Box 2249
Oak Park, IL 60303
866-443-7987
www.marionstreetpress.com

To my wife Janet for her love, support and inspiration
                                          — *Robert Reed*

To Melanie, my wife and best friend.
                                          — *Glenn Lewin*

Contents

Introduction

Why Business News is Important

Robert Reed

Gone are the days when only the corporate elite or Fortune 500 executives devoured the financial pages. Now, it's everyone into the pool. Why? Because for every Donald Trump, there are millions of small investors, owners of family businesses, women and minority entrepreneurs, young people who are starting their own enterprises, retirees opening up consulting firms, and everyday job holders.

These people are also readers, online users, viewers and listeners. In ways that we may not realize, business is an undercurrent to nearly every major civic and political debate, an integral part in determining our quality of life. Name it: access to health care, improving education, urban revival, suburban sprawl (not to mention what we eat, wear or do) and each topic has a business angle worth examining and bringing out in the open.

"Business news has moved from the back of the sports pages and in between the stock tables to become Page One news. Its part of the mainstream now," says Martha Steffens, the Society of American Business Editors and Writers (SABEW) chair of business and financial journalism at the University of Missouri.

What's more, in this era of technological wizardry — when the Internet eradicates borders, when everyone can "go international" with the click of a mouse and when new means of communicating are being implemented every day — there's a greater hunger and need to understand what makes the local, regional, national and global economies really tick and explain how they're dependent on each other.

Introduction

The task of examining, comprehending and stating clearly what business is doing, and the ramifications of its actions, falls to the journalists who cover business. It also depends, more than ever, on strong local content and coverage. Every community is touched, in some manner and degree, by business news and events (whether it happens at home or abroad) and local news operations have a greater opportunity, and responsibility, than ever to fulfill a unique journalistic and public-service role.

The goal of a strong local news operation is to bring compelling stories "home." That calls for great work, not just copy to fill space between advertising. Ideally, it means producing hard-nosed, aggressive coverage of local business issues, companies and personalities. And it means developing a healthy skepticism bolstered by a skill set that can dig into and comprehend the myriad facts, figures and agendas behind every business story. Once done, that information must be distilled and then presented to readers in an informative, powerful and, yes, entertaining manner.

The mission of this book is to provide journalists with an edge. It will help newsroom managers build strong business reporting and writing staffs, which will embolden them to set their own lively agendas — one that goes beyond massaging wire stories and giving into the relentless pull to just feed the news-hungry beast. For reporters, it will unlock the secrets of pursuing the story, getting that all-important interview and presenting information in a manner that draws reader in and keeps them wanting more.

And hopefully, the fruits of these combined labors will provide readers, users and viewers with the business news, information and analysis that a free society needs to make informed decisions.

Chapter One

Build it and They Will Read

Robert Reed

Let's face the facts: Journalists aren't the world's best planners, organizers or managers. Some skeptics go so far as to say they wouldn't want a journalist to run a bath.

There's a reason for this: Planning, organizing and managing can be incredibly boring, and action-oriented reporters and editors didn't get into journalism to be bored. They like the chase, reacting to events and rushing to meet a deadline. It's in the DNA.

Still, when building, or improving, business coverage it's important to repress those instincts enough to create a "working philosophy" that can propel coverage and provide a sense of purpose and direction to those toiling in the vineyards of business news departments, and to those reading the fruits of their labor. Even small newspapers can benefit from a solid philosophy about business coverage.

Any successful working philosophy requires an organization to take a tough look at itself. Not always an easy or pleasant chore. It would be great if readership surveys and research were available (and when they are use them), but most news organizations aren't inclined to go that way, either because they don't want to spend the money needed for such self-examination or because they recoil at the thought of doing any market research. So, tapping research is often a moot point.

Also, working philosophies — if they are to really work — need "buy-in" from a news organization's major in-house constituencies.

That includes top-level business-side leaders (publisher, owner, etc.); top editors or newsroom managers; news department heads; business section editors or leaders and assistant managers. Moreover, it must be a philosophy that a newsroom leader can quickly articulate to staff and, most important, to the readers (or viewers, listeners and online users) and sources within the community.

To do all this means holding a few meetings. It also means confronting some difficult situations and doing some institutional soul-searching. Among the questions that a news organization must ask itself:

■ Will the section speak to business people or will it strive to reach everyone?

■ What's missing in our approach now?

■ Will coverage be limited to print or will it seriously expand into online, TV and radio?

■ How can we distinguish ourselves from competitors?

■ Are we willing to pay the price for more aggressive coverage?

■ What happens when our coverage angers or alienates an advertising department's "sacred cow" — big employers, auto dealers, retailers, real estate interests or grocery store chains?

Among these, the biggest question is: Who is the section's primary, or ideal, reader? I believe local business sections should first be geared toward the business person, entrepreneur and personal investor (someone with money in stocks, bonds, mutual funds, etc.). The section must be sophisticated yet highly accessible to all these readers. That means stories must be on the cutting edge, jargon-free, written in a compelling manner, and aggressively edited to exceed the readers' high expectations.

Let's be clear about an important point: This does not mean that a newspaper's business news section should become a glorified trade magazine, nor a business-to-busi-

> **One mission statement:**
> "The business section goal is to be the area's premier provider of business news and information in print, broadcast and online. It will break news, cover and analyze major business trends and happenings, while also providing much-needed perspective and greater insight into the economic events affecting our community. It will also serve as a resource and sounding board for the area's workers, investors, decision-makers and those impacted by business decisions."

Avoid paralysis by analysis

Only hold a few meetings. Don't fall into the trap of "paralysis by analysis." No one can anticipate everything. So, enter each meeting with the explicit intent of hammering out a philosophy quickly. Do what's required of journalists: Set a deadline, stick to it and move on!

ness publication, similar to the business weeklies that populate most markets.

Nor does it mean passing over or downplaying business stories that affect the public at large. Quite the opposite: Corporate corruption, massive lay-offs, outsourcing, the global economy, and other so-called "business-to-consumer" news greatly affects everyday readers and merits more page one, or upfront section, presentation. These are the stories that allow the business staff's work to break out of the business page or section and leap onto page one.

Indeed, a business news staff that's really on the ball and understands what makes commerce and companies tick can add tremendous value to those stories and give the entire news organization a competitive edge. Don't be satisfied reporting the facts of an event ("Company XYZ is firing 5,000 employees"), but strive and drive to explain why something is happening and what it means to the community. Most of the time, the company announcement is only the tip of the story. There's always more.

At the end of this "working philosophy" process, a news organization should produce a one paragraph "mission statement," a viewpoint that will simply, clearly and easily state why the business section exists, sets priorities and outlines what it will strive to accomplish. That may sound geeky or too MBA-ish for rogue reporters and hard-boiled editors. But it doesn't have to be that way.

It's not enough for an editor, or even a group of them, to have an idea in their heads or to "know good coverage and ideas when I see it." That's not leadership. Strong and effective newsroom managers continually state their goals, so all involved know what level of expectation and performance is required.

Remember, the mission statement is not meant to be a bouquet of flowery prose and ideals (leave that to the head of the entire organization), but rather a set of goals that drives coverage.

Chapter One

Brick by brick: building staff and coverage

Every local business news department is different. Those with a lot of resources have the luxury of picking and choosing their staffs, either from the news organization's existing pool of talent or by going outside of the organization to lure experienced people. Smaller news organizations don't always have the clout to add or attract staff, so often they have to hire and mentor younger, less experienced, journalists.

Whatever the circumstances, hiring and crafting a business reporting and editing team is tricky business. In fact, most editorial managers will concede that the toughest part of their jobs is hiring the right people. With that in mind, here are a few guidelines:

■ Leadership — The business editor is the news organization's business news expert. We'll assume that any worthy job candidate has the right stuff to be a newsroom leader: Brains, competitiveness, curiosity and creativity. It also helps to have someone with the political chops and smarts to deal with the paper's bosses. These are the qualities every news organization is looking for in every staffer.

I'd argue that these attributes are even more important when covering the complex economic and commercial worlds.

Moreover, it helps to bring a blend of experiences to the job. Someone who can only see a story's business angle may not realize the wider impact that such events have on the community. A sharp business focus is good, myopia is not. It doesn't serve the reader or the news organization.

That said, it is preferable for the business editor or leader to have a good grasp of what makes the economy and the financial markets tick. That's because nearly all business stories, no matter how complex or mundane, will ultimately be viewed through that prism. If a company closes a factory, it's because something has happened in the economy to bring that about. If a CEO is indicted, chances are some shareholders have been scammed.

This is not to say every business editor has to be an MBA or investment whiz. But it helps to have this background going into the job (along with the other traits mentioned).

Remember, other business disciplines or beats can be learned over time, but a strong basic understanding of finance and markets will help even a relatively new business editor quickly get up to speed.

■ Assistant leaders — A given: You'll want deputies with good news judgment and editorial skills. But before hiring or promoting someone, it helps if the business editor is honest about his or her own strengths and deficiencies. The business editor may sparkle at story development and big picture projects but be a disaster at implementing a plan, moving copy or handling operational matters. Look for someone who brings complementary skills to the department. Assistants should not be mirror images of the business editor. Hire people who will challenge without becoming obstructionists to implementing the section's plan.

■ The troops — Some of the most important people on any business staff are the reporters who go out and bring the stories back.

Ideally, a reporting staff will be a blend of veteran and less-experienced reporters. The theory is that experienced reporters need less direction (and management's time) and know where the bodies are buried, while greener reporters can often bring a fresh point of view to their assignments (but require more mentoring).

On top of that, it helps if the reporters have had experience covering other types of stories before moving over to business. Having worked a City Hall beat, covered cop shops and courts, honed in on features that deal directly with everyday people is a real bonus.

Try to avoid hiring someone directly from a trade magazine who lacks any general news gathering and writing experience. Someone who thoroughly understands a specific business beat (and has contacts) may have advantages, but if that reporter has never been "on the streets" covering other news and coping with many different situations, it's likely that reporter will have more trouble, or at least need more time, adjusting to the demands of writing for a mass audience or providing a broader range of coverage.

Hiring help

Over the course of my career, I've worked in at least 10 different newsrooms, large and small. They include: trade magazines, community and daily newspapers, radio and television and a regional business weekly. As a newsroom manager and editor, I've interviewed, hired, promoted and fired numerous editorial staffers. Happily, most of those I've hired on a permanent or free-lance basis worked out, but some did not.

Chapter One

What to look for in a job candidate

■ A journalism degree. Yes, some of the world's best reporters and writers never set foot in a J-school. But know what? A lot of terrific people have journalism degrees. There are many great journalism and communication schools in this country and my bias is toward those who've attended them, show a commitment to the craft (perhaps with an internship or two), have an idea of the job demands and possess some feel for the role of the press in society.

The right hire can have an undergraduate J-degree and an advanced degree in another discipline, unrelated to journalism. Or vice-versa. I've found that chances for success increase (especially when hiring entry-level reporters with limited real world experience) if they have a J-degree.

■ Experience: For entry or mid-entry level, there's the usual bill of fare: internships, work at a college newspaper or broadcast station, part-time work at a media company. All good stuff. But there's more. What type of global experience does the job candidate bring? Has she traveled to other parts of the world or is she open to doing so? What type of personal journey has he taken before becoming a journalist?

It takes all kinds. One of the best business reporters I know ran a clay pottery business before entering the newspaper game. She didn't have a J-degree but worked her way up through community newspapers before becoming part of a major daily paper's business new staff.

Others have worked for a while in Corporate America as lawyers, salespeople or managers before taking the leap. Some had blue-collar jobs in industry (I'm one of them). In all these cases, the question managers must ask is: What made you switch to this business? If you like what you hear, it could lead to a good hire.

■ Skill set: Look for job candidates who aren't afraid of numbers and know how to befriend them to tell a compelling story. They don't have to be math wizards, and much can be learned on the job; but if numbers scare them, find someone else.

■ Attitude: Look for someone with a healthy sense of competition, someone who doesn't like to get beat on a story and hustles. That said, remember that some balance is needed. A reporter or editor who must win at all costs can end up violating ethics and hurting everyone involved.

Bottom line: The same skills that make a good police, schools, government, or metro reporter are also what make a great business reporter. When you find someone with talent, curiosity and a good attitude — hire him or her. And then fight to keep him or her, too.

Critique, please

So you've honed in on a worthy job candidate. The clips look good, references check out, and the job prospect even interviewed well. It's time to make an offer, right? Nope, not just yet. One more important step should be taken before that occurs. Get the candidate to write a critique of your section, maybe even the newspaper. This is undoubtedly a pain for both the job candidate and the employer, but it can provide great insight into any hiring situation.

Some organizations ask the prospect to do the critique near the beginning of the interviewing process, while others ask for it near the end. Either way, tack this one on somewhere in the process and make sure all the key hiring editors review it.

Why bother with all this?

There are a couple of reasons. First and foremost, it shows if the job candidate can actually write. Don't laugh. There are many times when an editorial candidate interviews well, has good clips (which some kind editor or J-school mentor helped craft) but can't write clearly. Secondly, a thoughtful critique can give the employer a window into the job candidate's reporting abilities. Can this person think critically? Ask the right questions? Back up assertions? Comprehend the news organization's broader mission? Test management?

Management should give a job prospect feedback on the critique. This will give the employer a sense of how the candidate reacts to editing and critical comment. And it gives the job prospect a feel for whether management wants to hear honest comments about the good, bad and ugly of the organization or just wants people to parrot the company line.

Here is an example of a critique, written for a senior management position with a major daily newspaper. The newspaper's name, and some other specifics, have been deleted. But this will give you an idea of what a critique can cover:

Here is my critique of the business section. I looked at samplings from four days, which include Sunday/Nov. 23; Friday/Dec. 5th; ; Monday/Dec 8; and Wednesday/Dec. 17.

...

Chapter One

CONTENT: For the most part, I'll confine my remarks to homegrown stories and not the wire copy pick-ups. However, I will note one stark contrast in the section is the difference in quality between the wire service stories and the locally-generated stories. In many cases, the wire stories are more deeply reported, sourced and speak with greater authority than the locally-produced stories. They are often better written, too. An important management goal will be to help bring the staff-generated stories up to a higher level, one that rivals and exceeds contributions from other news outlets. Another goal should be to limit the number of national, wire-service stories in each section by replacing them with good local copy.

By that I don't mean going overboard and ignoring breaking or spot national news that has local impact. But why use a wire story on labor shortages (Monday/Dec. 8) on page one of the section? The impending labor shortage is an important story (one that also has a nice counter-intuitive hook during this "no job growth recovery") that can and should be written from a local perspective (using the national data as a backdrop to the story but also striving for local data).

Page one anchors: Let me be blunt — some of these features are a mess. More troubling, they are prime examples of good ideas that fall flat because of poor execution. "Company XYZ names new chief" is an example.

This story does not speak with authority, nor does it strongly tee up what the new CEO is going to do or what he's up against. Indeed, the lead is almost retrospective, not forward-looking, and the bulk of the story explains what the previous CEO did (spin-offs, etc.) which is old news.

What's needed is value-added analysis.

How will the new CEO improve margins? What is HIS strategy? What type of guy is he? What's his management style? What does labor have to say about him?

Yes, he'll continue to focus on "factory automation," which strikes me as code for closing expensive U.S.-based plants, opening facilities offshore where costs are cheaper. But he's got to do much more. He must refocus the entire company.

It appears he's going to make it less dependent on selling manufacturing goods by moving Company XYZ deeper into the (allegedly) more lucrative management consulting business, primarily overseas.

In the lingo of the computer age, the hardware maker becomes a software provider. This, it seems to me, is the lead and the thrust of the story but it never comes through. It's also a very risky strategy, although you'd never know it from the story.

The story should focus on how the new CEO is going to change the company. Not that he got the job. The readers will already know that by the time they pick up the paper. And no reporter should ever fall for that company line that a new CEO is just going to carry on the previous CEO's strategy or plan. To do so, is career suicide — especially at a publicly traded company.

...

Non-anchor stories: These news stories are sound workmanlike efforts but nothing to rave about. My biggest concern is the lack of context and authority.

For example, the "Rise in health care costs smaller in state" misses the boat.

It seems to be telling readers that an 8% hike in premiums is okay because the rest of the country is paying more. The fact is that 8% is still a whopping increase at a time when inflation is below 3% and is nothing to cheer about.

Hit that angle hard: Employers will once again be hit with hefty premium hikes that will force them to revamp, or perhaps discontinue, the type medical coverage they provide workers.

Moreover, what are the ramifications of this increase? I bet it will mean employers cutting back coverage, raising deductibles, or switching carriers. The story makes a nod to those possibilities but does not address them head-on. Nor does it address small business, which is probably paying 10-percent-plus (small firms always pay more than larger companies.)

...

STORY MIX: Basically, the weekday sections display good, solid story mixes. Not always a lot of energy and excitement. I don't sense a great deal of personality in the section. The one column I saw was sort of lost on the page. Moreover, while I like business briefs on the cover, the newspaper has too much of a good thing.

Cut down on the number of them and prioritize them better. The reader wants you to be the editor!

STORY PLACEMENT: My bias is clear. I prefer strong local stories in the lead spot. For instance, I would have played up the (major local retailer's) dismal November numbers story (and used it as a way to look ahead toward holiday shopping trends) instead of the Washington-based steel tariff story. More people shop than buy steel, eh?

DESIGN: I like the use of photos for the anchor stories which take the reader into the workplace. The graphic on the hospital room story also serves the reader, giving them a quick look at how the rooms are and what they could become. I would have tried to use another color besides green, something more striking that could hold the graphics together better.

Generally, I like the design of the pages, although the issues I saw tend to have the same look. I think mixing it up more will help generate excitement, as will the use of more charts. More packaging of news, art and graphics will do that too.

Pillars of support

Every business newsroom needs some basic resources, such as the Internet, Bloomberg, reference materials, and a budget for subscriptions.

■ Get a Bloomberg. Without a doubt this is a nifty machine. The "Bloomberg" terminal provides an almost boundless amount of pertinent information. Stock prices, market capitalizations, major institutional investors, corporate history, market updates and background. It's just the ticket, especially when toiling on deadline. Depending on your budget, Bloomberg can be expensive. The company offers a stripped-down version to small news organizations and prices are set on an escalating scale. For the basic service of the news wire, some extras, and one Bloomberg terminal, a small newspaper with circulation under 50,000, for example, pays $400 per month. For a newspaper or magazine with circulation between 50,000 and 99,999 it's $500 a month; for 100,00 to 149,000 it's $750 and beyond that $1,000 a month. The more extensive Bloomberg, with all the analytical bells and whistles, costs more.

■ Internet sites. The World Wide Web is an invaluable source for background information for corporate information, contacts, background and more. All editors and beat reporters should have a short list of "go-to" business-oriented web sites that they click on every day for news, information and updates. Some must-haves for general news: Marketwatch.com (used to be CBSMarketwatch until acquired by Wall Street Journal owner Dow Jones Co.); CNNMoney.com; The Daily Deal (a subscription-based site with some free content); Hoovers (for company backgrounding); Yahoo Finance (a good digest for general business news); The Street.com (interesting take on Wall Street mindset); Briefing.com (which monitors the markets and trading trends at different levels and costs). Access to company-related blogs and message boards usually makes for fun reading, and perhaps some tips, but they have to be thoroughly checked out.

(WARNING! Read critically and check out what doesn't strike you as correct. Also, remember nothing replaces talking to real frontline sources and real people. The Internet is a supplement, not the whole informational diet.)

Also, while these sites are a great resource, remember that there is a built-in lag time and some of the information is not presented in "real time."

■ Subscriptions. With the Internet there's probably less need for trade magazine and other print products that can assist a beat reporter. Staples: any direct competitors, the Wall Street Journal, USA Today, The New York Times, Business Week; Forbes and Fortune. For the globally-minded, the Financial Times.

Chapter Two

A Biz Editor Who Means Business

Robert Reed

What's the bane of middle management? It's too much responsibility and not enough power. Often, that's the uncomfortable zone many business editors (who are mid-level managers) can get bogged down in.

For them, the challenge is to successfully manage past those nagging constraints in order to get the most out of their staff and their own editing experience.

For some up-and-coming newsroom leaders or careerists, being a business editor may not be the pinnacle. It may just be a stop along the way to bigger assignments. That's OK. Whatever path is taken, a truly engaged business editor can develop a deeper and wider perspective into his community's powerbase and the power brokers who influence it. That's a view few other editing positions can provide.

More important, an effective business editor is a catalyst for action, hopefully for the betterment of the news organization. Here are some tips on getting the most out of the demanding business editor gig:

■ Don't be a know-it-all. The title business editor doesn't mean you're the oracle of all that is business-related. Yes, it's important to have a solid base of knowledge, a comfort level with commercial and financial concepts, and a basic understanding of numbers and corporate strategy. But commerce is ever-changing, so it's important that the section editor embrace the job as a learning process.

■ Do cast a wide information net. Read everything, in print and online, about business that time allows. A regular diet should consist of The Wall Street Journal, The New York Times, Fortune, Forbes, Business Week and Barron's. The Financial Times and Economist are also great resources. But also check out the established news weeklies, selected Internet sites, and other non-traditional sources of coverage like the muck-raking Mother Jones magazine.

■ Don't waste time reading nitty-gritty annual reports, SEC filings and other financial disclosures of major companies covered by your news organization. You're primary job is to think big picture.

■ Do encourage your assistant business editors, team leaders and reporters to delve into this data and information, which is often

Who's your biz editor?

The duties of the business editor often vary with the size of the news organization.

It's rare to have a "business editor" at local broadcast outlets, although some of the larger radio stations use that title to showcase their on-air financial reporter.

In print, it's a different story. What follows is just a thumbnail description. Every business editor brings his or her own special skill set and experiences to the job. And every news shop has its own quirks and ways of doing things.

Small newspapers: At small local newspapers (dailies with circulation under 100,000, weeklies or semi-weeklies) it's not uncommon for the business editor jobs to be picked up by a managing editor or assistant managing editor. They are responsible for other parts of the paper of which the business section (perhaps a page or section front within another section of the larger paper) is one of their many jobs. This typically calls for showcasing wire stories, or slotting stories with a business angle that are written by general news staff.

Medium-sized newspapers: At mid-sized newspapers (circulation in the 250,000 to 300,000) there tends to be a separate business editor who's responsible for more administrative and staffing duties. Recruiting, hiring, firing all play a role. Also expect to do a lot of "managing up." That entails taking part in daily editorial budget meetings

a fount of story ideas, tips and angles. Tap into their knowledge with frequent, but informal, meetings designed to talk about story ideas, concepts and trends.

■ Do be an in-house advocate for your section and stories. Fight for your right to Page One space or the top of the broadcast. These battles are won, and lost, in the budget meetings with other section leaders and the top editorial brass. Go in prepared to answer the basic questions, the most important one being: Why will our readers care about this story?

■ Do connect with the community. Don't avoid the people and places you cover. Push yourself to attend business functions, take meals with business people and experts, invite CEOs, advocates,

with other senior and section editors and pitching stories for front page play. Typically, this editor reports to the managing editor or an assistant managing editor. Depending on the publication's commitment to covering business (and how story-rich the business community is) there's typically a staff of eight to 10 people, made up mostly of reporters but also with a couple of assistant business editors or a Sunday editor. Some newspapers have dedicated copy desks or graphics desks for business news: others let it flow into a universal desk that handles other sections. In this capacity, the business editor does a fair amount of hands-on, deadline editing and graphics brainstorming.

Large newspapers: At bigger newspapers, the business editor may also carry the title of assistant managing editor and be over an assistant business editor and a number of special editors responsible for selected coverage areas and stand-alone sections on real estate, autos, etc.

A staff of more than 12 reporters is not unusual, with each covering one or two specialized beats. In addition to overseeing the business news department's operations and "managing up," this editor is often the public face of the newspaper in the business community and beyond.

It's not uncommon for a major business news department to have a number of assistant editors who oversee in coverage of various topics (technology, health care, service industries, manufacturing and agriculture) and work closely with beat reporters, from the assigning to the editing stage.

small business owners, etc. over to your news shop for background talks and moderate an occasional panel for industry groups (but do not take payment for this). In short, become the personification of your organization's business news coverage.

■ Don't get co-opted by business or commercial interests. Business editors have to walk the fine line between covering the business community but not being part of it. That means keeping arms-length from trade groups, business-backed initiatives, civic endeavors, and do-gooder causes that want to be associated with your news organization. Chances are, you'll be dealing with a lot of people who make a lot more money than you. Don't be intimidated or envious of them. Play it straight. And if your news organization doesn't have an ethics policy, get one.

■ Do be the "go-to" person for upper management. Practice the fine art of managing your bosses. Have and display a base of information and working knowledge on all things business so your bosses, and fellow managers, seek you out when a business-related question arises within some other section or department's zone. It could be local news, sports, international coverage or any other beat because, as we've said earlier, commerce touches every walk of life.

■ Do be an advocate for your readers and audience. This is your most important task. At the end of the day, that's what the business editor job is all about. Manage, edit and lead with them in mind.

Teeing up, but not teeing off, the reporting staff

Where can a business editor add value? Oddly enough, it isn't in the grind of daily coverage. While being a great wordsmith and copy doctor are terrific skills, the business editor has to bring something even more important: A vision of what each major story is and a knack for getting staffers to produce, and improve on, that idea.

This does not mean dictating a story theme to a reporter. And it certainly doesn't mean hyping facts and figures to bolster a preconceived premise or notion. It does, however, call for the editor to serve as guide and to work closely with a reporter, checking in with him or her during key points in the fact-finding and writing process.

Sounds time-consuming? It doesn't have to be, provided editor and reporter understand the process and can develop a quick and candid communication method, whether in person, over the phone or via emails. I call it "upfront editing."

■ Talk it over. Whether it's big breaking news or a major enterprise story, take a little time to talk to the reporter about what's happening, and just as important, try to flesh out what it all means. It's here that a little planning can go a long way. For example: When you know that the giant Company X is going to report earnings the next day, have a chat with the beat reporter about how crucial this quarter is (or isn't). Ask what Wall Street's consensus is and discuss what it means if Company X makes it or doesn't. Discuss what the angle for the story may be in either case and press for context. Arm the reporter in advance: Tell her not to just digest the numbers and results, but to probe for reasons behind those earnings and determine what the proper context (competitive, marketplace, etc.) is needed to view them honestly and properly.

■ Check in. It's okay to check up on a story as it's happening. Most reporters are dying to tell someone (even their editor) what's up. This is a great time to provide some important input or take corrective measures should the original premise the reporter and editor hashed out fail to hold up. Recognize holes in the reporting and push for more info, or pump up the volume by adding resources. Indeed, the story may be so good, or have so many compelling angles, that two or more reporters should be on it. Now is the time to act, not when the story hits the desk.

■ Time to write. The rubber meets the road when the story is being written and edited. As editor, you want to minimize surprises (unpleasant ones, at least) and those have a way of popping up during the writing process. Read over the reporter's shoulder (if there's no union rule saying you can't) and make sure the story is headed in the direction that both editor and reporter have scoped out. Even the best business reporters can take detours as they start to write a story, and it's the editor's job to keep them on track. Check out leads, make sure all the important bases are being touched, and check to see that the tone of the story isn't too timid or belligerent. Make sure key numbers and statistics are part of the story mix — and are used to back up business reporting assertions. A good business editor must nudge, coach and encourage the reporter to address all the important points raised during the "upfront" sessions.

■ Time to rewrite. The story is good. Now make it better. If that means kicking it back to a reporter (even on deadline), then do it.

Aggressive copy editing

The best thing any business news section can have is an aggressive copy desk, whether it's a stand-alone copy desk dedicated exclusively to business coverage, or is part of a universal desk that handles copy for all sections. Here are some tips constructing a crack copy editing team:

■ Hire copy editors who want to edit business news. You wouldn't have someone edit sports if they hated the subject. The same reasoning applies here. Granted, filling any copy editing job can be daunting, but make the necessary effort to find copy editors who have an appetite and appreciation for business news.

■ Time to go to school. Many times, copy editors are told they'll learn while on the job. I'm all for hands-on experience, but business news requires a different skill set and expertise than editing politics, sports or features. Chances are that we all vote, play games or go to concerts and movies. As a result, we have a connection to those experiences and that makes it easier to edit stories about them. But how many journalists (especially those just out of J-school) have run a business, made a payroll or even purchased some stock? News organizations can save themselves lots of grief and embarrassment by insisting that copy editors attend business tutorials and seminars (offered by professional associations such as the SABEW or the American Press Institute [see page 29 for details]). Also, have local experts from area accounting firms, business schools, or local banks stop by and give short classes on various business concepts.

■ Empower the desk. Reporters need to know that they cannot bully copy editors by saying "that's an industry term" or "our readers will know what I mean." Good copy editors are a reporter's best friend. They make stories better by checking names, titles, numbers, and insisting on the proper context. Most important, a business editor must make it known that the copy desk is there to test, quibble, nit-pick and make copy the best it can be.

■ Make numbers clear. One of my pet peeves is that numbers are so badly reported in too many business stories. It's not only that they are wrong (there is a difference between a million and a billion), but that they are often used without the proper context. It's not enough to report a company's earnings are up 50 percent without providing a timeframe. As a rule of thumb, copy editors should go on red alert when they see numbers in a story. Check the number with the reporter and, when possible, ask to see the original or primary source from which that number originated.

■ Kill the jargon! Some business journalists think that a liberal use of industry terms lends greater credibility to their stories. Actually, it's just the opposite. Clarity is the goal. Jargon is clarity's enemy. Copy editors must aggressively strike down jargon, insist that terms be defined and explained to the reader. (See the jargon sidebar on page 102.)

Graphically speaking

Business coverage does not always make for the most compelling art. But nothing brings a dusty business tome to life like a strong photo or graphic presentation. Here are some other considerations to keep in mind:

■ Think photos. The best business photos are of people doing their jobs. Think of the subject of a business story the same way you would star athletes — get them in their natural environment. True, an airline CEO may be a desk jockey. No matter. Strive to get that CEO in an airline setting — in the terminal, baggage claim area, or even in a cockpit.

■ Big-time CEOs hate to have their pictures taken. Chances are the CEO of a Fortune 500 company won't have the time, or inclination, to take a creative picture. So what? Go for it! Even if you fail to get the photo that was originally envisioned, you may end up getting something close. One thing's for sure: It will be better than a portrait of a man in a blue suit and red tie sitting behind a desk.

■ Entrepreneurs like to have their pictures taken. Small business owners and operators love publicity and are usually willing to do whatever it takes to attract attention. Since entrepreneurs don't have to report to a board of directors (like CEOs do), they tend to make their own decisions and just plow ahead with a photographer's concept.

■ Graphics work. The judicious use of numbers, charts, infographics and other devices can add an important journalistic element to any story. This information is part of the story and just as important. To achieve the best graphics, the art department and reporter must work together. Reporters should know what numbers or statistic their coverage hinges upon. They should flag the art department early in the process, providing the information needed to build a graphic. Remember, even the most elementary stories can benefit from the basic "pie" chart or a graphic of a stock price that charts the 52-week highs and lows. There's an art element to every story — you just have to recognize it and then present it in a clear, clean fashion.

■ Simple is better. Graphics that are over-loaded with numbers, percentages, and market share figures tend to work against themselves. In this case, simple is better. Often a clear-cut look at an important statistic (an annual profit chart, for instance) makes a powerful case.

■ Illustrations. Sometimes, photos won't work, nor will statistics. But an illustration will, especially on major editorial projects. Illustrators tell us that their best work comes out after they have had an in-depth discussion with the reporter about the story. If the reporter can describe the essence of the story to the illustrator or art director, it can translate into some great eye-catching illustrations.

Help!

Here are some resources to help your newsroom produce better business copy:

■ Yes, math is intimidating. But with some basic understanding, you can navigate most business news events with relative ease. Luckily, help is available.

To start, buy a copy of "Math Tools for Journalists" by Kathleen

Woodruff Wickham (Marion Street Press, Inc.). An invaluable primer on the language of numbers, how figures are used, how to understand and present them to the everyday reader.

For more advanced information, read "Understanding Financial Statements: A Journalist's Guide," by Jay Taparia, a certified accountant and MBA (Marion Street Press, Inc.).

To order these books, call 866-443-7987 or visit www.marionstreetpress.com.

■ Career enhancement: Tap into organizations dedicated to offering courses or seminars dedicated to providing working journalists a greater understanding of their craft and the business world. Here are a few industry groups and resource centers worth checking out on a recurring basis:

Society of American Business Editors and Writers (www.sabew.org). This not-for-profit group is headquartered at the Missouri School of Journalism at the University of Missouri-Columbia. SABEW offers a variety of seminars and special programs designed to inform and improve business reporting. Also, the SABEW site provides "Internet Links and Online Resources," an array of business, industry and economic sites that are worth listing under the "favorites" category of your web browser.

The Donald W. Reynolds National Center for Business Journalism at the American Press Institute (www.americanpressinstitute.org). API is an increasingly important resource for business news organizations of all sizes and stripes. Once at its web site, check out the BusinessJournalism.org site, which provides a wealth of information, including in-depth interviews with some of the country's leading business reporters.

The Poynter Institute (www.poynter.org). This is a school for journalists based in St. Petersburg, Fla. It offers a variety of support services and while not solely dedicated to business reporting, it does have a number of seminars and speakers who can address that type of coverage. It also showcases the great Romenesko journalism site, which taps into all the breaking news about the industry and more (find out if your boss is staying or going). Moreover, it is home to www. journalismjobs.com — the web site where news organizations nationwide post job openings, including many business reporting and editing gigs.

The Knight Center for Specialized Journalism at the University of Maryland (www.knightcenter.umd.edu). For 17 years, the Center has provided free high-quality seminars in law, health, science, energy, finance and many more topics to journalists. Unlike some other fellowships that require months of study (which can be a great way to recharge your professional batteries or enhance careers) these seminars are for short spans of time, a week or couple of days. (Full disclosure: I was among the first Knight fellows in 1998.)

Chapter Three

The Beats Go On

Robert Reed

In an era of convergence and overlapping interests, it may sound blasé to say that old-fashioned "beat" coverage is still the best method for covering (and breaking) news. But it is. Most business news departments, no matter what size or scope, should rely on strong beat coverage and management.

The essentials

These are business beats that are so pervasive that no local newspaper section can thrive without them. They cut across every walk of life, touch everyone either as a consumer, employee, investor or citizen. They have impact on a community. They are:

Real estate - commercial

The use of land for office buildings, industry, retail or a combination of all these is one of the lynchpins of business news coverage. Every community has some type of development story (or stories) going on. Examples:

■ Hot growth areas cope with the strain of new office towers popping up all over.

■ Established urban centers fight to remain commercially viable without tearing down older, architectural gems.

■ Open fields in exurbia are being plowed under to make way for industrial facilities and speculative "build-to-suit" industrial parks.

■ Communities decide whether to attract or repel super-sized retailers like Wal-Mart, Target and others.

Real estate - residential

Many of the same arguments that apply to commercial real estate apply here. One difference: Residential real estate coverage hits people closer to home — literally. This coverage seeks to chronicle the way people live, where they live and how they live. It means covering:

■ New housing developments.

■ The rebirth of depressed areas through public or private redevelopment efforts.

■ The quest for affordable housing.

■ The opulence of living large and the onslaught of mansions, or McMansions, in many of the nation's suburbs and cities.

■ Mortgages, taxes, and lifestyle choices.

Sacred cow alert: Many newspapers depend on their weekly residential real estate sections for advertising revenue. While many of these sections play it straight, others go soft on residential housing developers and real estate interests. Any news organization that aggressively covers, and uncovers, residential real estate news should be prepared to face the occasional slings and arrows of outraged advertisers.

Retail

Everyone shops. Some run to the malls, others click a mouse and buy online. There are few business relationships that consumers take more personally than shopping. Whether it's going to a "big box" discount chain for bargains on everyday items, or to an upscale boutique to make a special purchase for a once-in-a-lifetime event, the retail experience touches us all. More than that, retailers have personalities of their own. An aggressive superstore may be welcome in some communities and scorned in others. Look at Wal-Mart. Likewise, a string of small, charming shops can revitalize a lackluster commercial strip but the opening of an adult book store along a commercial street can have an entirely different effect. Increasingly, stores have become "village centers," meeting places and gathering points for an increasingly mobile, often rootless, society. In short, with the right approach there are lots of good stories to be told under the retail umbrella.

Sacred cow alert: Remember what I said about those residential developers and real-estate interests? The same rule applies here. Only more so. Local newspapers depend heavily on retail advertising, whether it's national or local clients, and those companies are not afraid to use their clout to influence coverage.

Health care

Just as everyone shops, everyone gets sick. Health care coverage is one of the most important subjects a section can cover. It's also one of the most confusing and challenging. The range of coverage is often mind-boggling. It includes medical centers, doctor practices, drug companies, private insurance providers, state-backed insurance plans, research and development, bio-technology, at-home care and much more. Out of this, every news organization will establish its own set of priorities. Health care reporters may never really know how the entire system works (who does?) but priorities should be established. If there is a major medical center or research institution in town, cover it. If there is a large group of people in your area affected by a disease or who can benefit from new research and drugs, that's where the stories are. As the Baby Boomers age, health care coverage will become even more crucial.

Financial services

Right up there with health care is the coverage of banking and financial services. Business sections are about following the money. Everybody banks, finances a car or mortgage, and uses credit cards. Increasingly more households have some money in the stock or bond markets. In some situations, news organizations with major banks or financial players located in their coverage areas will report on what those institutions are doing. This typically calls for reporting on strategies, high-level personnel changes, and community-oriented stories (lay-offs, philanthropic giving, etc.). With industry consolidation (especially in the banking business but also in insurance and investment banking) that type of coverage is becoming less pervasive simply because there are fewer stand-alone community banking and financing groups.

Tailor made

A business news organization should also develop a unique set of beats, something that goes beyond the basics just outlined. Often it reflects an industry or service business that is headquartered locally or otherwise has a major impact on local readers. These beats reflect a region's way of life or reason for being. For example, a Los Angeles news organization will cover the entertainment industry in ways a Midwestern daily will not. And a Midwestern newspaper will cover agri-business, or manufacturing, more aggressively than the West Coast news organizations. And Detroit-area news groups will cover the auto industry more intensely than news organizations in other parts of the country.

Every region has its own group of business and economic concerns and it's important for the local news organization to recognize and go after them. Often, these coverage areas are where a news organization distinguishes itself.

Some examples:

Manufacturing

The Rust Belt continues to be the heart of manufacturing. Nearly every major news organization in the Midwest dedicates resources to covering this shrinking, but still important, industry. However, this coverage does not need to be limited to the Rust Belt. In the 1980s, auto manufacturers, and their vendors, began opening plants, service centers and distribution outlets in other parts of the country. So even though manufacturing may not be a top priority, it is possible that some manufacturing-related activity is going strong in your area.

Agriculture

Coverage of the Wheat Belt and Corn Belt and food producing industries can touch almost any region. But coverage does not have to be limited to farming. Food processing, distribution and safety, and commodities pricing are all ingredients in covering agriculture. Covering the "food chain" can make for some great stories.

Gaming

Not everyone gambles but nearly every state is getting into some form of legalized gambling. While Las Vegas and Atlantic City have cornered the market on huge casino action, gaming is definitely moving into Middle America. Not only are more publicly traded companies opening up gaming venues, Native Americans (who are allowed to run casinos on their land) are a major force. All of this comes on top of other types of legalized gaming, such as government-backed lotteries and horse racing.

Transportation

People and goods have to move. One of the most important, and daunting, jobs facing a company is to get its goods and services into the hands of customers. To do this, Corporate America takes to the air, roads and rails. Moreover, people have to get from point-to-point and how they do it is a story worth telling. Airlines, airports, air/rail/trucking transportation centers, trucking, shipping ports, etc. are sources of great stories. They range from straight business coverage (management, labor financing issues) to broader topics, such as security.

The business of government

Over the years, the business of government has become a hot area to cover. A former employer of mine, Crain's Chicago Business, was among the first weekly business publications to branch out and cover city, county and state government as a business. Money is, after all, the mother's milk of politics, and by focusing on the business of government, Crain's broke numerous stories on pocket-book issues pertaining to budgets (and budget fights), taxation, corporate fees, contracts, expensive lobbying initiatives, privatization of services and many hot regulatory issues. To add value, such stories were infused with a healthy dose of political reality — telling readers which contractor is connected to City Hall or some state office, who profits from quietly-made zoning changes, who's getting fat off the expansion of government-backed facilities, such as O'Hare International Airport, or the money pouring in to lobby for expansion of Illinois gambling (a regulated industry).

Such coverage provides a window into who's doing business with the government and what it costs taxpayers.

Chicago is a hotbed for such coverage. The Chicago Sun-Times recently did an award-winning series "Clout on Wheels" that chronicled a scandal-ridden hired-truck program backed by Mayor Richard M. Daley's City Hall. It was a masterful blend of business and political reporting that has resulted in scores of indictments and the dismantling of the program.

Technology

Someone call tech support! Technology is driving the world, so it helps to have someone who can connect with what's going on. In California's Silicon Valley, tech coverage is essential. In Chicago, where there are fewer home-grown technology companies, it may not be as intense but it's still important. The advent of the Internet, new generations of computers and other wizardry, and the growing dependence on technology for most every type of transaction (business or personal) make this a key coverage area.

Tourism

Not every town, city or state is a tourist destination. But areas that heavily rely on tourism or conventions (an increasingly competitive industry) should concentrate their reporting firepower on this area.

Good, but not essential

In the best of all worlds, a news organization can cover everything. A handful of them can. But most cannot, so some hard decisions have to be made about where to spend resources and energy. Here are some areas that are worthy of coverage but not full-time staff and resources:

Small business

Here's a hint: Most small-business people and entrepreneurs don't think of themselves as "small-business people." They consider themselves part of an industry or the economy. Cover those stories and you will touch their lives. For the most part, issues that touch big business — taxes, regulations, financing, etc. — also affect small companies. There are some unique areas, such as estate and succession planning, but frankly those can be handled on a spot basis and don't require major commitment.

Personal finance

There are only a handful of good personal finance stories out there. Basically, they are variations of some larger themes, including: How to pay for your lifestyle, how to save for retirement, how to manage a portfolio, how to handle or pass down an inheritance. There is a need for good personal finance sections, but it's not necessary for a local news organization to spend limited resources on a full-time personal finance reporter. There's plenty of syndicated and wire copy out there, which can, with a little creative editing and lay-out, fulfill the mission.

The markets

This may sound like heresy to a business editor, but your section does not need a dedicated markets reporter. That is NOT to say your staff should be populated with people who find the markets a mystery. Everyone on board should know the basics, be aware of the stock movements of publicly traded companies, and make every effort to be market savvy, especially in these fast changing times of 24-hour trading. But a dedicated markets person to report on the ups, downs and nuances of the market every day is not necessary. There's plenty of syndicated copy to do the job.

Other optional beats

Economic development,

The beat memo

Taking over a beat? See if there's a beat memo. Good newsroom managers will ask departing or transferring reporters to write "beat" memos that serve as outlines for continuing coverage. A good beat memo doesn't need to include information that is readily available from other sources (like the ones just mentioned). But it should:

■ Identify the hot topics for companies on the beat.

■ Tell which companies are up or down and the major issues each is facing.

■ Provide reliable industry contacts. Who's worth chatting up. Who's an empty suit or a waste of time. Names, numbers, email addresses, etc. are always welcome.

■ Reveal the personality of each company or nature of the industry. Do they cooperate with the press or hate its guts?

Keep in mind, the shelf life of any beat memo is very short. But in the beginning it can be vital in helping a newbie reporter get to know the beat and its players faster and more efficiently. It's also a nice way to help out a colleague.

non-profits/charities, sports marketing, media and marketing, Washington D.C. It would be terrific if a newspaper covered all of these areas with strong beat reporters. Each can produce big-impact stories. But a local newspaper can draw from other departments' resources (national, metro, sports, features) to cover these topics. Great stories, with added dimension and sophistication, come when insightful journalists from these non-business sections team up with good business staffers and blend their expertise into strong coverage.

Chapter Four

Covering the Corporation

Robert Reed

It's essential to realize that no beat, company or institution stands alone. It's all part of something greater — a community, industry or economy. A journalist's goal is to pierce that world, understand and uncover what makes it tick, and then report back to the readers.

Chances are there is at least one large publicly traded company in your main beat. Here's how to get started covering it:

■ Don't freak out. Yes, Company X is a global concern, or the area's largest economic engine. So what? It can still be conquered (from a reporting perspective). Go into this beat with an attitude of entitlement. Be confident, but don't be rude or self-important. Just remember you have every right to ask questions, seek answers, hold the company responsible for its actions, and use every honest means necessary to find out what's going on.

As a young banking reporter, I had lunch with the chairman of a large local savings and loan that was coming under fire from federal regulators. Unlike many crooked S&Ls, this one had not done anything wrong, but its capital level was deficient (the government had raised thrift capital requirements as part of its massive S&L bail-out package). During the lunch, the CEO made clear that he was going to have to sell the company or it would be taken over by regulators. Neither choice thrilled him and he wasn't happy to talk about the situation. But, because I had done my homework and was aware of his company's plight, its growing need for capital, the new S&L reforms

Be a Corporate Profiler

Nail down the basics. Find out what the company does, if it's publicly traded or privately held; who has a large ownership interest; what it makes or does; where its headquarters and major subsidiaries are; who runs the place and what their standing or reputation is within its industry and communities.

■ Tap into the company's web site and really drill down into all this information; go to web sites like Hoovers or Marketwatch.com to get basic profile and financial information.

■ Do a LexisNexis search of major trade and general publications. Go back five years or so for context.

■ Remember to plumb the archives of your own publication. See what your predecessor wrote. If you can, debrief the reporter who covered the company before you.

and related industry havoc, this CEO was willing to talk and was candid. I got a scoop and also laid the groundwork for future stories about the fate of the company, which eventually was acquired by a global banking power just before a government takeover.

■ Background check. Editors will often tell novice reporters to just "start calling people and ask them what's going on." That advice may work on general assignment beats, but don't rush to do that on a business beat.

A more productive approach calls for doing some quick but effective research before hitting the phones or knocking on a CEO's door. Knowledge is power. Use it to draw more information from sources, recognize better angles and capture the best story. It's also essential in developing sources and tipsters. So, hustle to get as much basic and timely information as time allows.

Pull down the last five years or so of the company's annual reports and read the narratives for any major personnel, strategic or financial shifts. Even if you don't know all the ins and outs of corporate finance, this is the place to begin (see more detailed information on reading financial reports in Chapter 6). Do an extensive LexisNexis search on the company, pulling up all major articles from the major financial publications. Don't limit your search to only your publication or news organization (and if it's a company with global interests, check out the overseas press coverage, too).

Search Amazon.com or other booksellers for any corporate biographies of the company or executives. Sure, many of these tomes are glorified sonnets to their corporate subjects, but they can provide historical information, and a glimpse into the company's collective mindset and culture. That will prepare you for what comes next. This may take time.

The idea is to get a grasp on the top-of-mind issues that pertain to your assignment. Search for answers to these types of questions:

■ Is the company making money? That's simple enough to check. But then delve deeper by making some comparisons:

● How does its return on operations compare to previous years?

● How does it compare to direct industry peers (those companies of comparable size or product mix)? Better, worse or in-line? Often industry experts will keep a record of how each of the companies they cover is doing and will publish those reports for investors. Get on their mailing or email lists.

■ How does it stack up to the entire industry it competes in, when weighed against some benchmark standard? For example, if a semiconductor company's stock is up 5 percent for the year but the entire Philadelphia Semiconductor Index is up 7 percent for the same time period, ask why. There are plenty of industry indexes out there keeping tabs on various sectors, including energy, retail, airlines and more. Periodically check those indexes and see how they're faring versus the company you cover.

■ What are its financial trends in terms of sales, earnings per share and stock price?

■ Is it under pressure from government, regulators, shareholders, activists or other stakeholders?

■ Are there any large outstanding legal or social issues affecting the company's actions?

■ What's its current business strategy? Has it changed?

■ Has there been a corporate regime change?

■ What's the company's standing within its industry?

Putting in some extra time to answer these questions helps build a solid base of information and will pay off.

Now, make some calls. After this preliminary fact-finding tour, you're bound to have more questions than answers. This is a good thing. Chances are the names of sources and contacts will pop up in this examination. Make a list of them and their expertise or background. Then, start digging by calling industry sources *outside* the major companies on the beat.

Think of a company or a beat as the center of a hub. Many businesses and services feed into this hub. For example, Oak Brook, Ill.-based McDonald's Corp. is at the center of many multi-billion dollar industries. Besides selling Quarter Pounders, fries and shakes billions of time over, it is also one of the biggest users of global agricultural products and commodities; among the world's most significant real estate holders; one of the country's largest employers (domestically, second only to the armed forces); a major independent franchisee operation; and a huge client of various legal, financial, marketing, political lobbying and other support services. And don't forget competitors. Sometimes Burger King or Wendy's knows what

The Outside Connection

Sometimes the best information about a company comes from external sources, such as:

■ Former or retired employess of the company you are researching (especially anyone from the sales or marketing departments). Locating retired employees is not as difficult as one might assume, as many list themselves as consultants with their industry trade groups. When conducting research in the rubber products industry, I was able to utilize a number of retired engineers to piece together the potential viability of a newly developed rubber.

■ Association directors/managers. Each industry is served by at least one trade association. Developing a relationship with the director or manager of a trade association can valuable, as these individuals are often at the crossroads of information on industry companies. One of the first industry research projects I undertook was in the flooring industry. All of the background and "big picture" sales and marketing information for that project was obtained through contacts established with the wood flooring trade associations.

■ Editors/writers for trade association publications: The editors of trade association publications are almost always aware of trends and new developments within their industry, and very often they can provide contacts to sources within the company you are researching. A recent example comes from the printing industry, where I was able to obtain an overview of new technologies and their impact on distributors and suppliers of film and pre-press proofing supplies.

■ Personnel recruiters: The industry jargon for recruiters is "headhunter," and these individuals are often the first to know what is occurring within their industry. As an example, executive or management

McDonald's is doing before McDonald's mid-level managers know it. And vice-versa.

McDonald's is not alone. Every company has a similar make-up. Just remember, every enterprise is the sum total of its parts. (See the sidebar above for a list of potential external sources.) Get a feel for this universe and then start calling up, or meeting, people within these sectors for background interviews. Eventually, they will go on record, but at the start of the process let them get to know, and trust, you.

If managed correctly, these people can prove to be great sources for tips, perspective and important reality checks. Sure, some of them

recruiters usually hear about layoffs before announcements are made to the public. The more a recruiter is tied into one industry, the more likely he is to have inside information. Look for specialists, not generalists. While conducting research in the aerospace industry, one recruiting contact had heard that a U.S. aircraft manufacturer was about to lose a contract to a foreign manufacturer. This information was obtained two weeks before it was announced to the public.

■ Industry consultants: Each industry is served by an army of consultants, most of whom have held management or executive level positions within their industry. Consultants are universally loyal to their clients, but will often speak "off the record" if asked about the industry as a whole, or about companies for whom they do not provide services. An example of this was a story I wrote detailing questionable business practices relating to Internet marketing. One extremely helpful quote came from an Internet marketing consultant who explained why the program offered by the target company could not possibly succeed as advertised.

Other sources you should consider include:
■ Regulatory agencies
■ Consumer activists
■ Suppliers
■ Vendors
■ Customers
■ Industry analysts (who can walk you through the numbers and strategies)
■ Unions
■ Shareholders, including individuals and portfolio or pension fund managers (who have a stake in the company but are not beholden to it)

— Reed/Lewin

may have axes to grind (that's part of the game), but by connecting with a healthy array of them, an enterprising journalist can get a much fuller picture of any corporation.

■ Go to the company. Now, start calling the company and get some face time with key executives. Chances are your first stop will be corporate public relations. PR people have agendas, too. They'll being taking your measure.

They'll want to know: Are you going to be a push-over? Or are you a hard-ass? Do you know your stuff? Can they make top executives available to you and trust that you'll understand (if not necessarily agree with) what's being said?

The company may even offer you a tour of the company, or headquarters, and give you a feel for their way of doing business. If it's offered, take it. You want to talk to key people — department chiefs and the CEO. Get to know the company and its decision-makers. That's key to building strong, sophisticated coverage.

Delving into the PR person's mind

Attitude, attitude. Reporters think of public relations people as obstructionists, toadies, spinners and liars. PR people view reporters as arrogant, ill-informed, biased and lazy. Can this marriage be saved? Sure, provided both sides get beyond those extreme views and do their jobs effectively. So lighten up and learn.

It takes all kinds. In the course of a reporting career, you'll find there are good PR people and lousy ones. Some PR people push to get their companies and bosses in the news. Others see their task as doing the exact opposite. No matter what the mission, one thing is always certain: PR people are not paid to be a reporter's friend. Still, by understanding the role PR people play in a corporation's culture, journalists have a better shot at connecting with the CEO and top brass — which is the objective.

They aren't waiting for you. No matter how large the company, the PR staff isn't sitting by the phone waiting to answer your call. Just like many news organizations, PR departments have consolidated operations, trimmed staff, and forced middle management to double up on duties. As a result, PR staffs are becoming more selective about which reporters they respond to and which ones they're going to ignore.

First among equals. Which news organizations do major companies believe are crucial to telling their story? In this age of stepped-up corporate accountability, companies have to be careful about playing favorites when it comes to releasing financial or other material information. Still, there is a pecking order. PR professionals say the first tier includes: The Wall Street Journal, New York Times, major wire services and the hometown newspaper.

Some companies' upper-tier includes broadcast arms like CNBC or CNN if they want to get the word out to investors fast. Corporations will always talk to the business magazines, Business Week and Fortune, but those publications are doing more long-form journalism, not breaking news.

Yet, even major dailies in large cities where the news-making company has a large presence (but no headquarters) may not always get a call back, or will be referred to a wire story or the company web site for comments. The second tier often consists of influential publications or national online sites, such as CNN/Money.com or Market-Watch.com, and selected trade newspapers or magazines. For example, a major retailer will

Your friend the spokesperson

An effective corporate spokes-person can help you out. Here's how:

■ Provide good backgrounders. They may talk off-the-record, or not-for-attribution, and provide a reporter some detailed perspective and information on a corporate situation or event. Reporters can then use this information to build their expertise and go back and ask for on-the-record responses.

■ Point you in right direction. This is the era of web-casts and analyst conference calls, but you'd be amazed how many reporters don't listen to these broadcasts. They are a treasure trove of executive quotes and information. Instead of saying "no comment," corporate spokes-people can point to comments and statements that upper-management made to investors.

■ Confirm if your story, or angle, is on the money. Asking a PR person if a hot tip is right is definitely a leap of faith. But there are times when a company spokesperson can wave you off an embarrassing angle (embarrassing to you and your employer) and explain why it ain't so. However, this is a delicate situation and should only be the call of last resort. Do this only after you've already vetted the tip and checked it independently.

reach out to Women's Wear Daily, while an advertising agency will connect with Advertising Age, say corporate spokespeople.

Down the line are community weeklies, peripheral trade magazines and small dailies.

Be an impact player. While the pecking order is a fact of life, here's another: Companies will provide access to smart beat reporters who are persistent and honest. It takes time and effort, but reporters who've worked the beat can get beyond the canned press statements and spin-control. Having done the preparatory work described in this chapter, you are a journalistic force to be reckoned with. As a

Go beyond the corporate press release

An example: In November 2004, Sears, Roebuck and Co. and Kmart Corp. entered into an $11 billion merger. To read the company statements at the time of the deal was announced, you'd never realize that this is one of the most complex mega-mergers in the nation's history. Nor is one told by the companies that this is a deal with far-reaching ramifications for a wide constituency: the retailers' investors; customers; employees; vendors and the thousands of communities nationwide that house their stores and headquarters and depend on them for tax revenues.

These are issues that the business news team is expected to uncover. The first thing an editor must realize is this is a story with "legs"—the impact goes beyond just saying the two retailers are getting hitched.

The first order of business is peeling back the deal and getting to understand who's buying whom, for how much and what is the currency (stock and cash? stock only? cash only?)

In this deal, Kmart acquired Sears by paying Sears shareholders in a combination of cash and stock in the newly formed company, Sears Holdings Corp.

Once the mechanics of a deal is understood, ask the next big question: "Now what?"

It's a short but vital query that often opens the door to many other intriguing questions that propel better coverage. It also fosters exploration of issues that can add value and substance to coverage of any merger or major transaction.

Find out:

■ Who will be the real power behind this new company?
■ Who will own the most stock?

result, the CEO and company will want to explain their side of the story to you.

Relationships. Like anybody, public relations people and their staffs want to be treated politely and fairly. Don't come off like your time is more valuable than theirs. There will be a time when deadline looms, but when it doesn't show some patience. Indeed, massaging a source the right way can pay off when a big story breaks. The right word from a subordinate to a busy corporate executive can help you get an important call-back when you're on deadline. There were many times I got such a call from major companies (airlines, banks,

- Who will actually run it and lead the executive team?
- Is there a culture clash waiting to happen, or a clash of egos?
- What does the balance sheet look like?
- How much debt will the company carry?
- Where are the cost-savings?
- Who in upper management is going to leave?
- Who stays?
- Who gets rich?
- Who gets shafted?
- How many job cuts will it mean (fyi: mergers always mean lay-offs)?
- What does it mean to customers?
- What brands will live, and which will die?
- How many facilities will have to be shut or revamped?
- How much damage will the loss of stores, factories or other related units cause to their immediate communities?
- Will it make the new company more competitive with industry leaders or hinder it?
- Don't forget Wall Street. But don't just check the deal out with industry analysts who cover the companies' stocks prices. Check in with institutional shareholders (mutual funds, pension plans, foundations, etc.) and see what the bond rating agencies have to say about the link-up. Also, if the state or city ever provided any tax increment financing (TIFs) or subsidies, see if the taxpayer can expect a rebate.

None of this is going to be in the corporate press release. Business editors and reporters have to know where to go and how to get this information. All that begins by not accepting what companies say at face value.

consumer product companies and more) because the support staff put a good word in for me at the right time.

Entering the corporate citadel

OK, you're in. It's time to interview the top person. Here are

The art of the executive interview: 5 rules to the game

Because American corporations are strictly "top down" operations, CEOs are not only the leaders of the businesses they run, but very often the face, voice and embodiment of these enterprises. As a result, when a corporate executive submits to an interview, the reporter understands that this individual is the one person in that organization who is truly capable of speaking to any issue affecting or confronting the organization. However, CEOs of organizations large and small are frequently media shy and increasingly media savvy, making themselves available to reporters only when they believe it is strategically in their best interest.

As a result of these realities, the rules of the game are different when interviewing corporate executives, and there are a number of considerations a reporter should be aware when interviewing a company's president, CEO, CFO, CIO, chairman, or executive vice president.

Rule #1: Understand that someone in this capacity is granting an interview not because it will help you, but because they believe it will help them. As an example, Carly Fiorina, former CEO of Hewlett-Packard, made herself readily available to the national business press while she was pushing for the Compaq merger. After the merger happened, and especially after it was widely perceived as a mistake, Fiorina dropped from the headlines.

Rule #2: Know what information you are after, and be prepared. It's critically important that you do your homework because (1) you will, in all likelihood, get only one bite at the apple, so you have to make it count; (2) because your line of questioning will be much more effective if you come into the interview prepared and with an agenda; and (3) people are more likely to open up if they get the feeling they are speaking with someone who understands them and their problems.

Rule #3: Understand that regardless of the size of the organization they are running, corporate executives generally have robust egos, and are used to being deferred to. This creates a special challenge for a reporter. If one appears too deferential, one loses respect, and having some measure of respect throughout the interview is important. My some tips:

Have a plan. Go in there with a sense of purpose. You're there to get the most out of the interview, so don't squander the opportunity. Go in armed with three or four questions that you absolutely want answered or addressed.

solution to this challenge is to create a climate of respect, but always with a businesslike and professional approach. Early in my business research and reporting career I vacillated between being too aggressive (as a result of my defensiveness) and being too deferential (as a result of my not wanting to offend). As I gained more confidence, I understood that to be successful I needed to relax, stay focused, and maintain a businesslike and professional attitude.

Rule #4: Dress the part. Too many journalists — business or otherwise — dress in too casual a manner. One need not wear a suit (though it wouldn't hurt) but certainly a shirt, tie and classically tailored sport coat is, to me, a prerequisite. This is important because it helps to level the playing field. Additionally, if one feels underdressed, one is at a psychological disadvantage. The rule of thumb I have gone by is this: if I am interviewing anyone in a company, and especially if the interview is taking place on their premises, I wear what I would wear were I walking in for a job interview.

Rule #5: Be persistent in your questioning, saving the most potentially contentious questions for late in the interview. Understand that corporate executives — like politicians — often receive professional coaching designed to keep them from saying anything revealing or potentially embarrassing about the organization. When it becomes obvious that an interviewee is providing non-answers or simply hitting on previously rehearsed talking points, I pause for a moment, then ask the interviewee the following: "If you would like your customers and investors to understand three things, what would they be?" This gives the interviewee the opportunity to further push his agenda, but it also forces him to stop and think for a moment. And after he has answered that question — and I will give him whatever time he needs to do so — I then follow-up with "I think I understand what it is you are saying. Now, in the interest of fairness to these same customers and investors, can't you tell me why...," and then I complete the question. I find that this approach serves the purpose of getting the interviewee out of his rhythm, but in a low-key, unaggressive manner.

— Glenn Lewin

Be prepared. Don't go into this encounter starting from scratch. Do the grunt work necessary for an effective interview. You don't have to know every aspect of the business, but you have to know about major events, changes and strategies. And be current! For example, you don't want to screw up and ask about a major division or business line that the company has long abandoned.

Don't get bogged down. This is big picture time. Unless specific numbers or information is essential to keeping the conversation going, move on. If you get too specific, a CEO will end up sending you to some lower-level type for data or dates. Capture the opportunity to discuss big ideas, events, strategies and decisions.

It's not all business. This is a chance to take a measure of the CEO and connect with him or her as a person. Get some color. Ask about outside interests, hobbies and influences on his or her life. Some CEOs will wax on about family and interests, others will clam up immediately. Either way, you'll learn something about them.

Among my favorite experiences was interviewing Robert Crandall, then CEO of AMR Corp., the Dallas-Forth Worth-based parent company of American Airlines. Crandall has a formidable reputation as a no-nonsense type who doesn't suffer fools lightly. With his feet up on the desk, he pushed back in his chair, looked me straight in the eyes and proceeded to discuss the problems his airline and industry were facing, and how he intended to address them.

At one point he said the most important role of a CEO was arbitrating between strong managers and picking one's ideas, or recommendations, over the other. The trick was to do it without causing undue hard feelings and major executive disruption, he added.

He used the imaginary goal of "getting to the other side of a wall" as an example. One person might recommend walking around, while another would say break through the wall, he said. His job was deciding the best course. But what remained constant is the goal of getting to the other side of the wall, he asserted.

I left the interview knowing that Robert Crandall was not going to be swayed from his goals.

Telling the story

Here's a quick step-by-step look at how a business profile evolved from an idea to the printed page. It was a 2,000-plus word profile of NFL hall-of-famer and former Chicago Bears player and coach Mike Ditka, who is also a serial entrepreneur, national product endorser and a very shrewd businessman. The story appeared in the September 2004 issue of Chicago magazine, the Tribune Co.-owned monthly city magazine.

The idea: As part of the process of writing for Chicago Magazine, I pitch a few story ideas to veteran editor Richard Babcock on a regular basis. During these "upfront" editing talks, we determine if it's a story worth doing. Prior to pitching them, I do a LexisNexis check on the topics to make sure these are new ideas or angles being pitched.

The questions usually center on these issues: Are we telling the reader something new? Telling them something important? What's the unique angle or surprise element? Does the topic have multi-dimensions that add depth and weight to the story? Can it be told in an accessible, entertaining way? If it's a well-known topic (like health care, finance or a known personality) then what's new about this story?

Once Dick is satisfied that the story is a go, then it's up to me to bring it home.

The inspiration: Why do a Ditka story? It's not like he's a stranger. Nor when you think of business do you immediately conjure up Mike Ditka. But there were a couple of reasons: The column was timed for the opening of the football season, when interest is high (Chicago is a big football town). Ditka is well-known (and in some quarters revered), so it's a profile with immediate name recognition, a hook for readers.

Also, while many people know of Ditka's football accomplishments, few outside the world of sports know him as a businessperson. Why not fill them in?

The plan: The aim was to focus on Ditka's business world or, as many sources put it to me, "Ditka: The Brand." The story would examine his enterprises, putting him to the test of any other corporate executive or company. His football accomplishments were a secondary theme to the story.

I wanted to talk to Ditka. He's a great interview. And it's a much better story with him than without. Because he's a busy person, the first call I made was to his office to try and line up a conversation. Ditka is a fairly accessible fellow, but he didn't know me at all. But what I believe helped get some time with him was the fact that I made clear this story was going to focus on his business, not football.

In short, Ditka made a business decision to talk about his commercial interests with Chicago magazine. Talking to Ditka was great fun. But had he declined an interview, the plan was to move ahead on the story without him. There was enough information out there to work with.

The reporting: Started with the basics. I did an extensive internet search on Ditka to get some background. I read anything I could get on him from LexisNexis, ruling out the stuff that didn't pertain to the column. In this case, the plan was to get a sense of how many business activities he had been involved with. Throughout coverage of his sports career, there were many tidbits that helped provide a stronger base, including mentions of his endorsements, restaurants, network and local commentator jobs, products bearing his name and more. Once this spade work was done, I started looking for experts in the endorsements, advertising, and market research fields — people who had expertise in sports and celebrity endorsements. My quest was to find out what they thought of Ditka's role and effectiveness. Some of my questions: Did he improve or hurt sales? Was he a quick attention getter or more? How much did he cost? How much did he make?

Moving on, I started to focus on his business partners, people who had been in a room with him making deals or who had hired him. I asked: What's he like to work with? Is he honest? Is he difficult on the set? What are his terms?

Get some color: From there, I tried to connect with Ditka as a person. I wasn't trying to unmask the real "Iron Mike," but I wanted to get a sense of how he conducted himself in daily life, get a feel for his personal versus public persona. I looked up colleagues, buddies and business associates with mixed success. Some talked, others told me to get lost.

The interview: By the time I connected with Ditka, I had a pretty good idea of what his business picture looked like. As a result, I didn't waste his time with a lot of basic questions like: "What are you endorsing?" The conversation was able to move at a higher level than that. Knowing his gig as spokesman for a drug to treat male impotence was running out, I asked him why he did such a promotion in the first place and why his endorsement deal was nearing the end. In addition, knowing what he was doing saved time for the broader, and more interesting, questions about his business philosophy, deals, what he looks for when running a business and more.

In short, I respected Ditka's time by paying him the compliment of being prepared. Everyone gets more out of those types of conversations.

The recap: After all the work, I took some time to re-evaluate the mass of information I had. What was good? What was junk? What to keep? What made a good lead? Most important, did this story take any twists and turns that I have to pursue? Sometimes, you go after one story and uncover another that's even better. That wasn't the case here. I was ready to write and, of course, deadline loomed.

The writing: Every journalist has his or her own style, so that's not the issue here. But, good discipline often leads to the best writing. In this case, because I knew the story was about "Ditka Inc.," I stayed focused and did not wander off and start writing his biography or a tome about his football career. All I had to do was write something that passed muster with my editor.

Here's the result:

Ditka, Inc.
By Robert Reed
Reprinted with permission of Chicago Magazine, copyright 2004

When Mike Ditka was a young, talented, and not very well compensated tight end for the Chicago Bears, he once joked publicly that his boss, George Halas, "(threw) nickels around like manhole covers."

Papa Bear was not amused.

"He was so pissed off, he was all over me," Ditka recalls today. Halas fumed that he resented being the butt of a joke that made him look like a "cheapskate." Under the onslaught, Ditka tempered his remark. "Coach," he said, "you are thrifty . . . but not a cheapskate."

These days, Ditka, 64, doesn't have to worry about ticking off any single employer. For years, as a player and later a coach, it seemed as if he never met an endorsement he didn't like, lending his name to a proliferation of products and enterprises from hot dogs to a limousine service, rugby shirts, cologne, a sports bar, and a security firm.

Since getting canned in 2000 as head coach of the New Orleans Saints, Ditka has ostensibly become more shrewd about his image. And he's become his own boss, corporation, and profit center with an eclectic range of business interests that generate a million-plus dollars annually.

That image the straight-talking everyman who is also a proven winner attracted desperate state GOP leaders earlier this summer when they dangled the party's suddenly vacant U.S. Senate candidacy in front of him. Ditka's pause to consider the offer suggests he doesn't quite understand his image yet (though it's possible he was only using the offer as a handy way to polish his reputation — and hike his fees).

In any case, he has become one of the nation's best-known sports personalities over the past few years, far outpacing many accomplished athletes who have tried to make the leap from the playing field to the business arena.

"He's been very adept at reinventing himself," says Bob Williams, chief executive and president of the Evanston-based Burns Sports & Celebrities, which links professional athletes to commercial endorsements and speaking engagements and has lined up occasional gigs for Ditka.

Ditka's current deal roster includes: owning part of a namesake Chicago restaurant at 100 East Chestnut Street, in the Tremont Hotel; appearing during the football season on a weekly radio show on WSCR-AM and a Bears preview show on WBBM-Channel 2; serving as spokesman for Majestic Star Casino in Gary, Indiana; selling his own brand of cigars (hand rolled in the Bahamas); and hawking Levitra, a drug to improve erectile function.

A large chunk of his income flows from his role as a popular speaker who racks up about 50 appearances a year (at what is said to be a minimum of $25,000 a shot). As the football season gets under way this month, he'll be a regular analyst for the sports network ESPN.

And earlier this year he found time to act in a movie with Robert Duvall and Will Ferrell about children's soccer (Kicking & Screaming is scheduled to be released in fall 2005).

That's a robust slate of activities for anyone, but what makes it even more impressive is that Ditka does all this while attempting to play 54 holes of golf a day, weather permitting, usually at Bob O-Link Golf Club in Highland Park (his handicap is said to be around seven).

In the winter he takes his game and his business schedule to Florida, where he officially resides.

"He's a national brand name, no doubt about it," says Kevin Adler, vice-president of sponsorship and events for Relay Sponsorship and Event Marketing in Chicago. "He even has his own logo" — a Ditka caricature, complete with spiky hair and bow tie.

"Da Coach," or "Iron Mike," depending on your choice, appears to be entirely pleased with the way things are going. "I think more people know me now than ever before," he says. "I walk through an airport and 150 people say hello."

Despite their occasional run-ins over money, Ditka credits George Halas for helping him get into business. While playing for the Bears, Ditka sought to open a West Side bowling alley with some partners and asked Halas for a loan. As Ditka tells it, Halas declined to provide the money, but instead took him over to American National Bank, the lender that Halas used, and got the budding entrepreneur a loan at the same interest rate that Halas would have paid, which was lower than the prevailing commercial rate.

"He said, 'You're going to learn to be financially responsible,'" Ditka recalls. "He did things like that all the time."

Throughout his playing and coaching careers in the National Football League, Ditka never had an agent, preferring to work out contracts directly with his bosses. But being his own advocate didn't always yield a huge payday, Ditka concedes.

"When I was 21 years old, I was going head to head with the founder of the league [Halas]," Ditka says. "Whatever he offered, I took."

On the sidelines as the hard-charging coach of the Bears, Ditka's persona emerged in full crescendo, bolstered by the 1985 season when the Bears posted an 18-1 record and won Super Bowl XX. The blunt, gruff, clipboard-throwing and headphone-snapping demeanor may have ticked off his players (and ultimately his boss, Michael McCaskey), but it endeared him to fans and, ultimately, to advertisers and promoters.

"I didn't [seek business deals] consciously," says Ditka. "Most of it was a result of being in Chicago. In retrospect, I look at it football-wise... It's being part of a team that's won two championships in 50 years . . . as a player [the Bears won the NFL title in 1963] or coach."

Some of his deals and agreements just faded away, while others crashed and burned when business plunged — his first Chicago restaurant among them.

These days, Ditka is head coach of his own business team, a small enterprise that includes a longtime assistant, Mary Albright, who handles Ditka's schedule and helps field the sponsorship overtures and inquiries that keep popping up. He won't say how much he makes, though it amounts to a tidy income.

According to advertising and sponsorship executives, a role as spokesman for a national campaign, like the one for Levitra, can land a fee in the high six figures or low seven figures; regional deals for a major personality fall into the mid-five-figure range, depending on the length of a contract.

Ditka's speaking fees range between $25,000 and $50,000, according to information posted on the Web sites of speakers' bureaus that represent him. Even at the base $25,000 rate, he stands to make $1.25 million for about 50 appearances per year. An analyst for ESPN can make in the neighborhood of $300,000 to $350,000 a year, say talent agents.

Ditka says his current restaurant is successful enough that he's hoping to expand the concept, possibly opening up spots in Naperville and Lincolnshire.

What's more, he's seeking to distribute his line of Ditka-brand sauces widely in food stores. This year he is also backing a line of Polo-type shirts, shorts, and other casual clothing priced from $65 to $100.

What do companies teaming up with Ditka get in return? Local businesses want to align themselves with Da Coach's shot-and-a-beer, working-class Chicago persona. And they also like being linked to the halcyon Super Bowl era of the mid-1980s.

When the Majestic Star Casino sought to distinguish itself from the rush of other casinos and gaming operations around town, its brain trust zeroed in on Ditka.

"He's not only a Chicago icon, but a winning icon," says Troy Keeping, vice-president and general manager of the Majestic Star.

Nationally, Ditka's image plays into a different game. The rest of the country doesn't get teary-eyed at the memory of Super Bowl XX, nor does it canonize Ditka as the country's greatest coach. It does, however, think of him as a "man's man," someone who will tell you what he thinks and let the chips fall where they may.

"Everything about Mike Ditka says 'tough,' " says Bob Bernstein, executive vice-president and media director of the ad agency Foote Cone & Belding. "Look at his restaurant's menu — it has pot roast nachos . . . for dinner!"

Ditka claims he doesn't think about his image. "I don't know what credibility I have," he says. "But when I tell people something, they'll listen."

Yet Ditka himself carefully vets the opportunities and partnerships he enters. When asked to describe his favorite kind of deal, Ditka replies: "Ones without lawyers."

Of course, he uses lawyers and advisers. But he also reserves the right to cut red tape when negotiations get bogged down. For example, when the Majestic Star deal was facing a bureaucratic lull, Ditka invited the Majestic executives over to his house, where they hammered out an agreement.

"We cut a lot of legal BS out of the contract," says Majestic's Keeping.

And Ditka has swallowed hard and started working with an agent — Barry Frank, vice-chairman of TWI in New York — on some television deals.

On the face of it, one of Ditka's weirder career decisions was agreeing to promote Levitra, produced and marketed by Bayer Pharmaceutical and GlaxoSmithKline.

Levitra obviously wanted to tap into Ditka's forthright reputation. But let's face it: When one of your nicknames is "Iron Mike," you think twice before agreeing to do national television commercials on male impotence. Ditka says a couple of tutorials on the physical causes of the problem changed his mind.

"I didn't want to go out and start shouting, 'This is my problem,' " Ditka admits. "But as I started to understand the problem, I said, 'I'm stupid if I don't go and do it.' "

How effective is Ditka as a spokesman and celebrity endorser? Marketing people think he's good, but they also note that his appeal can backfire. He tends to get quick results. When he became a spokesman in 1999 for Consort, Alberto-Culver Company's hair spray for men, sales went up 23 percent during the first year of his four-year contract, says Williams of Burns Sports & Celebrities, which helped connect Ditka with the company. Eventually sales leveled off, but they remained ahead of their pre-Ditka numbers, Williams says. (A spokesman for Alberto-Culver did not return phone calls.)

The Levitra endorsement, on the other hand, appears to face some issues. Market research has shown that women often prompt their men to seek help, and Ditka's rough-and-tumble image doesn't connect well with the female audience.

"He crosses over well with white-collar and blue-collar folks," says Adler, of Relay Sponsorship and Event Marketing. "It's more dubious with younger folks and women."

Advertising experts point out that Levitra has changed its selling tactics by not using Ditka in its TV campaign (he still has a prominent promotional role on Levitra's Web site).

Now there's some doubt as to how long he'll be on Levitra's selling team, especially if its maker doesn't come up with more dollars.

"If I'm going to make a commitment for so much time, they have to be committed to me financially," Ditka says. (A spokesman for GlaxoSmithKline says it is still open to working with Ditka.)

On the lecture circuit, the NFL Hall of Famer could easily do more than the 50 speaking dates a year he now does. As with most speakers, Ditka's talks have a running theme. His hook is called "ACE," which stands for "attitude, character, and enthusiasm."

"I don't have all the answers, and I don't profess to be what I'm talking about," he says. "There's no such thing as a motivational speaker. . . You have to motivate yourself."

Still, those who have heard Ditka speak say he fires up grown men with a mix of inspirational and humorous anecdotes gleaned from his personal and professional life.

An unabashed conservative, Da Coach is a favorite with business groups, no doubt another reason the Illinois GOP tried to hook him as an emergency replacement for Jack Ryan. But Ditka apparently concluded that his style wouldn't transfer to the stump.

"I don't try to be politically correct," he says. "I refuse to be. A lot of people are making fools of themselves because they're saying things they don't believe."

For Coach Ditka, that would be a bad game plan. Not to mention a bad business plan, too.

Chapter Five

Business Research:
An Investigative Approach

Glenn Lewin

Not all business reporting is investigative in nature, but some of the most important stories have been told by reporters spending weeks or even months researching and nailing down supportable facts and information. One example from the recent past was the work done by Fortune magazine writer Bethany McLean to unravel what was occurring at Enron; in pursuit of that story she spent months researching Enron's partnerships from a financial, legal and management angle.

Most of us, of course, will never be in a position to uncover a major national story with far-reaching business and social implications (not to mention the acclaim and fortune that comes with writing the book and selling the movie rights). However, notoriety and fortune aside, there is a real sense of pride that comes with "getting it right." In my experience the most effective method used for uncovering facts is the investigative model, and in this chapter I will outline why every business reporter should be able to conduct an investigation, and how a proper investigation is undertaken.

Initiating the investigation

Imagine the following: a business reporter writes a two part piece on scams perpetrated against the elderly. In his piece he describes some of the most common scams perpetrated on senior citizens and what steps can be taken to keep from being victimized. In preparation for his piece he interviews police investigators, geriatric psychologists, and local prosecutors. The first installment appears on the front page of the Sunday business section. A few days after his article runs, he receives dozens of calls from elderly readers describing how they have been scammed for thousands of dollars from a company offering them a "turnkey" home-based business. Each of the victims had been told he or she needed only invest in the start-up costs required to initiate the sales effort; once the business was up and running, the checks would start flowing in. After hearing their complaints, the reporter is convinced that there is a story worth telling, or at least investigating. The reporter approaches his editor, who agrees to allow him time to initiate an investigation.

Investigative project reporting differs from daily reporting in the following ways: first, a reporter engaged in project work typically has more time to conduct research and pursue leads and contacts. Second, when conducting an investigation, one has a "target" to investigate, whereas in daily reporting one is simply looking to understand the story and tell it to the reader in a succinct and interesting manner. Third, reporters and editors have to be especially careful to not only nail down their facts and information, but also to report the full and complete story that those facts represent (i.e., to avoid shading the truth to fit a pre-conceived notion of what they assume the story to be). And finally, the process of an investigation differs from daily reporting in both scope and attention to detail.

As an example, if a reporter is writing about a company opening a new plant, that reporter will probably accept as fact whatever the company public relations department reports (i.e., plant size, number of new employees and the target date for the plant's opening). However, if that same reporter is investigating the company, she is much more likely to independently verify anything reported to her by the company spokesperson.

The investigative mindset

Regardless of whether an investigation is criminal, legal, medical, scientific, or journalistic in nature, the methods and attitudes employed by investigators are similar; and these include the following:

■ Every investigation should start with a clean slate. While an investigator may think he knows the story (which is why an investigation is launched in the first place), he must consciously remember that what he thinks he knows may or may not be the truth.

■ Investigators should be guided by facts. Investigators who fall into the trap of forcing facts into a theory do an injustice not only to the target of their investigation, but to the investigation itself. There are thousands of examples of police investigators who railroaded innocent suspects into prison simply because a detective thought he knew what had transpired, and pursued only those facts that fit the theory.

■ An investigation should be worked from the outside in. I refer to this process as "peeling back the layers of the onion." In a business investigation this means conducting interviews and background information first with those peripherally involved, then proceeding closer to the target. As an example, if the target of an investigation is the CEO of a privately held business, the investigator might start by conducting a public-records search of both the company and the CEO, then perhaps interviewing others in the industry, and proceeding from there. The fundamental objective of this process is to master the facts before ever approaching the target. When interviewing the target of an investigation, you may only have one opportunity, and it is imperative to do your homework in advance; this is what allows you to ask probing and relevant questions, and to pursue the story with effective follow-up inquiries. (See more on external sources in Chapter Four.)

■ Quickly establish rapport. The one single strength a reporter should work to develop is the ability to quickly establish rapport with his sources. This is done by finding common ground (maybe the reporter attended the same high school as his source, or perhaps they know some of the same people); being conversational, not coming off as an interrogator (nothing causes someone to throw up defenses faster than if he feels he is being interrogated or badgered); reassuring a source that you are not a threat; and listening to her with empathy and understanding (give her time to tell her story).

■ When researching a business, look for information resources that are within the industry, but outside the company. The following are all proven business information resources: personnel recruiters (commonly referred to as "head hunters"), association directors/ managers, writers and editors of trade publications, industry consultants, former or retired employees of the target company, and chambers of commerce or local business networking groups.

■ Make certain facts are supportable, and preferably from multiple sources. Facts are elusive creatures; what we think we know is very often different from objective reality. One can never be certain of a source's motivation. As a result, if a piece of information is uncovered that advances a story but cannot be independently verified, it is best to leave it out. When conducting an investigative report, my standard is to read the story sentence by sentence, questioning each fact and each quote. Any assertion made by either the reporter, a source or a document must be independently verifiable.

■ When conducting interviews with company personnel, start with lower level employees and work up the org chart. Lower level employees (such as sales reps) can be excellent sources for information. The advantage of starting at the bottom is twofold: first, it enables the reporter to add to her information mosaic in a low risk manner (few employees will report to a superior that they have been approached by someone from a newspaper); and second, if an executive takes exception to your questions, he may "freeze you out" by circulating a memo instructing employees not to speak with reporters. An example would be to interview Wal-Mart store associates in an attempt to determine what changes the company has announced in the recent past. After interviewing employees at the associate level, you have a starting point and can use those initial interviews as leverage when attempting to interview managers at either the store or district level (though in the case of Wal-Mart, you can pretty well be assured that formal inquiries will be met with a firm "no comment" and a call from their public relations people).

■ Be creative, seek out non-traditional sources of information. Valuable information may be obtained from internal company documents such as memos, emails or employee training manuals. Sources will, more often than you might suppose, provide copies of these documents, though they'll often ask that their name be kept out of the article. How these documents may be used is something a reporter must clear with her editor — and in many cases the managing editor as well. Additionally, don't assume that a memo or email is accurate just because it was provided by a source. Work to obtain independent verification of any received document.

Internal documents are most often supplied by either disgruntled employees, or employees who realize that something is wrong and want to do the right thing (and for this reason one must always be on guard against being used by someone with an agenda that goes beyond simply getting out the truth). Depending upon the state in which the reporting is being done, confidentiality may be a concern. A recent example is Apple's lawsuit against Apple Insider, Think Secret and PowerPage, three web log sites devoted to providing news and information on Apple and its technology. In its suit Apple charged that the information posted on those web sites was (1) proprietary in nature, (2) had to have come from an employee engaged in the product's development and — as a result — (3) that that employee certainly was in breach of their signed confidentiality agreement. As of this writing, Apple was looking for the web logs to reveal the name of the employee (or employees) who provided the information, and a California Superior Court judge ruled in Apple's favor.

■ Understand that all stories (and investigations) are about people, not organizations. It is the human drama that brings interest to any story. Two excellent examples are *The Informant*, by Kurt Eichenwald, the story of Mark Whitacre, ADM and that company's attempt to corner the lycine market; and *Soap Opera*, by Alecia Swasy, the story of Procter & Gamble's obsessive control and marketing arrogance. Central to the Enron story were Kenneth Lay and Jeffrey Skilling, and central to the collapse of MCI-Worldcom was Bernie Ebbers. Therefore, when investigating a story, focus on the characters involved, not the organizations in which they function.

■ Practice the art of leveraging information. This is another example of why it is best to work from the outside in. The more you know, the more you realize that information gathering is not a one-way street. Once a reporter has developed a body of knowledge, she may be able to take some of what she has learned and trade up for yet more information. Sources are more willing to share if they are let into the process; just be careful not to reveal too much — assume that anything you reveal to a source will make it back to the target.

As an example, if you were researching an industry to determine what impact foreign imports were having on its U.S. companies, you might interview a number of industry experts and employees from foreign-owned firms, then take that information and use it as a baseline of knowledge when conducting interviews with managers and executives of the U.S. companies whose story you are looking to tell. By sharing what you know with those you are interviewing, you will often find that your interview subjects are more comfortable and willing to open up because you have developed more of a bond of trust; plus, people are more willing to give once they realize it is not a one-way street.

■ Maintain an inquisitive nature, an assertive attitude and a thick skin. One fact leads to another. Sources frequently refer reporters to other sources. By constantly asking who, what, where, when, why and how, the reporter will invariably complete the mosaic. Assertiveness means not being intimidated by the target of your investigation. Remember: no one wants to be the target of an investigation, and once he discovers that a reporter is on to him, he may react with the threat of a libel or slander suit. It has always been my contention that it is better to seek forgiveness than to ask for permission. Investigative work is as much about attitude as technique, and the willingness to push on in the face of threats demonstrates both character and professionalism.

A case study: 'The most dangerous con man...'

An example of this type of business investigation is an article I wrote detailing an Alabama-based company offering a one-week "business seminar" designed to put entrepreneurs, inventors and small business owners in touch with investors willing to help fund their ideas and dreams. The seminar cost each participant $5,500, and was held on one of three hotel properties (two in Los Angeles and one in the Phoenix area).

In conducting this research, I followed the process of working the investigation from the outside in. Specifically, my initial phone inquiries were to a company sales rep, where I had her explain what service the company was providing, and how I might benefit from it. I received marketing literature from the company, which included a copy of their consumer contract (which they named their "student enrollment form"). This contract was over 3,500 words in length, and was set in seven-point type. After spending an entire Saturday reading and working to understand the contract, I presented a copy of this consumer contract to an attorney for review. In addition to providing me with valuable information, he was willing to allow me to quote him on some of the more interesting and important points of the agreement. The gist of the contract was that the "student" had no right of redress except through binding arbitration in Alabama (at the expense of the student), and if the student were to file any formal complaint against the company, the student could be held liable for breach of contract and sued for both defamation and the company's legal fees. Never mind that the contract was probably unenforceable (according to the attorney I had review it); the contract's real purpose was to intimidate anyone from even attempting to litigate were they to feel wronged.

My next avenue of inquiry was to contact the Alabama Better Business Bureau and the Alabama Attorney General's office to find out if the company had complaints registered against it. Both agencies reported complaints against the company, and the Alabama Attorney General's office was willing to forward my name to both complainants (the fact that there were only two complainants was of initial concern until I learned how the company, through its law firm, would threaten any dissatisfied customer with legal action). Both complainants, a man and a woman, contacted me, and both were willing to tell their story. The female student told me how the company had pitched her on how her business would "explode" were she to attend this seminar, and that they would put her in contact with "hundreds of people" interested in helping her to promote and advance her business.

When she arrived at the hotel and met the other students, she soon realized that all of them were attending for the same reason — none were investors offering to help small businesses. By the second day of the seminar she had felt betrayed, and had asked for a refund. She was denied under the terms of the contract. As a result, she stayed through the week, and collected as much information on the company as she could get. Part of this information included a series of directories that included the names, addresses and phone numbers of other attendees from her seminar and others held by the company. She mailed me copies of these directories, and using this information I was able to contact a number of other seminar attendees and obtain their stories.

After interviewing over two dozen randomly selected attendees from the directories, I found the same story over and over: that each had been promised access to investors interested in their business. Many of these attendees had asked for refunds after realizing they had been taken advantage of, and all had been denied and threatened — in writing — with legal action.

In addition to the interviews, I conducted documents research through incorporation records, tax records relative to the 501(c)3 filings (all non-profits have to make their most recent federal tax filings available to the public), and related public records. This research resulted in my learning that the company's president and founder had been incarcerated in federal prison on two separate occasions for business fraud. One of these occasions had been in the 1970s, and the other in the mid-1990s. Additionally, another reporter working with me on the story learned that this individual had a federal lien for over $1 million against his home in Alabama, as a result of a civil action initiated against this individual on yet another alleged business fraud.

An articles search led me to a story in the San Francisco Chronicle detailing this individual's arrest and conviction in the mid-1990's, which resulted in an interview with the U.S. attorney who prosecuted the case. He offered the opinion that this individual was "the most dangerous con man" he had ever prosecuted. After four weeks of digging, I was able to write a 4,500-word article detailing how this company preyed upon entrepreneurs and business owners seeking an opportunity to realize a dream, only to learn that there was essentially no chance the promises made would ever be kept. The final vindication of the reporting came when the company's attorney admitted they had no grounds for a defamation suit because I had nailed down every fact and confirmed every quote. The editor for whom I wrote the story called it a "textbook example of how an investigative project should be handled."

Investigative business reporting is more art than science. It very often entails hour after hour of tedious leg work and countless interviews — most of which go nowhere. It can be expensive and, if not pursued in a thorough and professional manner, fraught with legal peril. And an investigative reporter who has invested time and effort pursuing a story may lose his objectivity and not be willing to let it go if the facts fail to support his initial theory. However, despite the aggravation, frustration and tedium that comes with the territory, it's important to remember that getting out the story is important work that carries with it its own rewards. Because the Enron case became such a major story, former Enron employees got a slightly better deal from the bankruptcy court and the government.

In the case mentioned earlier of the elderly being persuaded to invest in a home-based business, the victims' only voice came from the reporters who wrote the story. Several complaints to authorities had not resulted in action; it was only after reporters became actively involved did law enforcement take notice.

Pursuing all business stories with an investigative mindset — paying particular attention to the verifiability of all facts, statements and documents — will improve the quality and professionalism of the reporting.

Chapter Six

The Paper Trail: Part I
Researching the financial documents of a publicly traded company

Glenn Lewin

Publicly traded corporations issue a class of common stock that is registered on a national stock exchange. Microsoft, IBM, Motorola, General Electric, Ford Motor Corporation, and AT&T are all examples of corporations whose stock is traded on the New York Stock Exchange.

When a company goes public there are a number of legal strings attached. The Securities and Exchange Commission requires periodic filings that are intended to inform both current and prospective investors on the company's activities. The amount of information required of a company is substantial; annual reports submitted to the SEC are often 100 or more pages in length.

The most commonly filed forms required by the SEC are the 10-K (an annual report), the 10-Q (a quarterly report), the 8-K (a report indicating significant changes) and the S-1 (a report indicating an initial public offering, issued when a company is taken public). When conducting background research, a reporter should know where to obtain copies of these documents, and what to look for when reviewing them. (See Using EDGAR below and Chapter Eight.)

Corporate executives employ public relations people whose principal job is to protect and preserve the company's image. Unless compelled by the SEC, company executives seldom release information that reflects poorly on their ability to manage. Therefore, it's incumbent upon the reporter to sift through the dissembling, spin and obfuscations in order to get as close to the truth as possible.

To determine if a corporation is publicly traded, one may reference the Directory of Companies Required to File Reports with the Securities and Exchange Commission (published by Bernan Press, Lanham, MD; www.bernan.com), by checking stock price listings in the Wall Street Journal or most any other major daily newspaper, or by visiting any one of a number of web sites such as Quotes.com and locating a company's stock symbol through the sites "lookup symbol."

10-Ks and annual reports

Simply stated, an annual report is a formal financial statement issued yearly. It must comply with reporting requirements of the Securities and Exchange Commission. Annual reports include the balance sheet, income statement, and cash-flow reports audited by an independent certified public accountant.

Annual reports are written to satisfy a wide array of readers, including stockholders and prospective stockholders, creditors, financial analysts, customers and suppliers. The manner and style in which the financial data are presented must conform to standards laid down by the Financial Accounting Standards Board (FASB), the Securities and Exchange Commission (SEC), as well as various committees of the American Institute of Certified Public Accounts (AICPA).

The financial information contained in annual reports is structured to allow readers in any state to review the report of any publicly traded company in any other state and use that information to make decisions on whether or not to purchase that company's stock, lend it money, or sell it products or services on credit.

A 10-K report is organized as follows:

Part 1
■ Description of the business.
■ Description of the property owned by the company.
■ Description of the legal proceedings in which the company is involved.
■ Discussion of matters that have been voted on by shareholders.

Part 2

■ Description of the company's common stock, including information on high and low prices, dividends, and number of shareholders.
■ Five-year summary of selected financial data, including net sales (operating revenues), income or loss, assets, long-term debt, and cash dividends.
■ Management discussion of the company's financial condition, changes that have occurred in the financial condition, and results of operations.
■ Financial statements, supplementary data, and auditor's report.
■ Changes in accounting principles and disagreements with the company's auditors.

Part 3

■ List of directors and executive officers.
■ Compensation of the executive officers.
■ Company securities owned by management and major stockholders.
■ Information on related-party transactions, including transactions between the company and management, its subsidiaries, and major stockholders.

Part 4

■ Exhibits, financial statement schedules, and reports on form 8-K.

The annual report to shareholders and the 10-K annual report are not the same document. A company's annual report, while being the document most major corporations use to communicate directly with shareholders, typically contains nonfinancial details of the business not reported elsewhere, as well as marketing plans and future forecasts.

The following is an example of what information may be obtained through a careful reading of an annual report. Kirby Corporation is a Houston-based publicly-traded company. Its stock is traded on the New York Stock Exchange under the symbol KEX. Kirby Corp. is in the marine transportation and diesel engine services industry. Operating a fleet of over 800 barges and tugboats, Kirby is the largest inland tank barge operator. According to its 2003 annual report, its total revenues were just under $614 million, with net earnings approaching $41 million, up from $27 million in 2002.

In their annual report to shareholders, Joe Pyne, president and CEO, and Berdon Lawrence, chairman of the board, provided the following information:

> In 2003, Kirby reported record revenues and the second highest net earnings in its history. These results were achieved despite continued sluggish U.S. and global economies, which continued to negatively impact petrochemical volumes, our core marine transportation market.
>
> Three significant strategic acquisitions played a key role in achieving our 2003 results. In January 2003, Kirby purchased the fleet of SeaRiver Maritime, Inc.... The second acquisition was October 2002 purchase of ten double hull black oil tank barges, and 13 towboats from Coastal Towing, Inc.... The third acquisition was the December 2002 purchase of 94 double hull tank barges from Union Carbide for $23 million.
>
> Kirby's cash generation remained strong in 2003, with net cash provided by operations totaling $112.2 million.

In reviewing its financial highlights and earnings, it appears that the company is experiencing relatively modest but stable growth and profitability. But that same shareholder report contains the following statements:

> Even though our financial results were favorable, 2003 was still a challenging year with only marginal cargo volume improvements seen in several of our marine transportation markets. As a result, we remained unable to pass through to our customers the true cost increases that we have incurred over the past three years.

In short, they are telling their shareholders that their primary industry is experiencing slow growth and increasing costs, and to retain market share they are unable to pass along cost increases. A more dramatic example of this phenomenon is in the airline industry, where the market is highly competitive, and the cost of fuel has put the squeeze on established carries such as United and Delta. If these conditions persist, they can have a long-term impact on a company's ability to compete. A reporter covering Kirby would logically follow up on this information.

> For 2003, Kirby's diesel engine services sector's revenues, operating income and operating margin fell to a three-year low. ... These lower results reflect a continued weak Gulf Coast offshore oil service market, a market depressed since mid-2001, and a weak Midwest inland dry cargo barge market, weak since early 2002.

Kirby's financial report indicates that its diesel engine services business accounts for 13.5 percent of its total revenues, which is a small but significant portion of its total business. It appears that the 3 percent downturn in revenues for 2003 over 2002 is the result of cyclical market conditions, as opposed to any fundamental problems in management. A business reporter could follow up on this information by learning more about why the offshore oil service and inland

Calling all reporters

Another way to learn about a company is to listen to the earnings conference call. These calls, arranged by the company's investor relations department and held quarterly, typically include the company president or CEO, along with the CFO, making their earnings presentation to major investors. A typical earnings conference call will open with a presentation by the company, in which officials discuss quarterly earnings and what events have transpired that affect earnings — as well as their expectations for earnings for the next quarter. The presentation is followed by a question and answer session in which investors query the company's executives on what has affected earnings and what actions the company is taking to improve earnings and maximize profitability.

The Internet affords the reporter the opportunity to listen to archived recordings of these conversations. Most major corporations now offer open access to archived investor conference calls through the "investor relations" link on their web site. As with understanding quarterly filings and financial statements, understanding the significance of what transpires during these calls takes time, effort and the desire to understand the nuances of what is contained in financial information made available to the public. Experience and practice are keys to gaining an understanding for what can be learned by listening to these calls.

dry cargo barge market are slow, and what the prospects may be for that market to turn around.

> Although 2003 was a difficult year, Kirby remains in great financial shape. Our investment grade rating and our $150 million revolving credit facility position us to continue to grow through acquisitions.

It appears as if Kirby is in a good position to maintain a market leadership position. A business reporter covering Kirby, however, might consider speaking with others in the industry to get various perspectives on Kirby's acquisitions and how they impact Kirby's position in the industry.

> Improved earnings, operating margins and returns will be partly led by higher volumes and some improvement in pricing, but will also be pushed by continued hard work on managing

Specifically, there is the opportunity to learn the business's fundamentals, as well as management's strategies and directions for the organization. The following are some of the key elements a business reporter should focus on when listening in on an earnings conference call:

■ Did earnings meet expectations? If they did not, how is management planning on improving earnings over the next quarter?

■ Did revenue growth keep pace with earnings growth? According to Mark Coker, founder of BestCalls.com, "revenue growth is the most important engine of future earnings growth and can help you determine if the company is gaining or losing momentum in the marketplace."

■ What is the attitude of management? Do they sound positive about future prospects for the organization, or do they come off as tentative and defensive?

■ Pay close attention to the question and answer session of the call; these exchanges are where information is revealed that you won't find in SEC filings or press releases.

■ Does management appear to have a good command of the facts? Are they able to readily answer questions, or are they fumbling for information and answers?

■ Are the current results in line with past-articulated strategies? In other words, are they executing their strategies as outlined in previous conference calls?

costs, working efficiently and managing our capital.

In this sentence management is telling its investors that market conditions are not likely to improve, but that the company will remain strong and stable as a result of its ability to manage the details of the business. Make no mistake, some of the best managed companies compete effectively by doing just that: properly managing the details of the business. But a good reporter will take some time to examine the premises behind these claims. How possible is it to manage costs? If the company were unionized, how likely would the union be to assist in reducing labor costs (traditionally one of the largest expenses for a business)? What does "working efficiently" mean? And how, specifically, is the company planning on managing its capital?

Each of the above excerpts show how information contained in an annual report can provide the reporter with a more complete understanding of the company's overall position within its industry, as well as providing avenues for inquiry and further investigation. The information contained in an annual report will not be as detailed as what is contained in a 10-K filing (Kirby's 2003 annual report, for example, is only 21 pages in length, while its 2003 10-K filing is 180 pages long). But as the Kirby example illustrates, annual reports contain generalized statements regarding current business operations, as well as what plans the company has to achieve growth and profitability in the immediate future. In that respect, annual reports offer a wealth of information.

Using EDGAR

EDGAR (Electronic Data Gathering and Retrieval) Online is a privately owned and operated database providing a comprehensive collection of SEC filings, including 10-Ks, 10-Qs, and 8-Ks. Documents are available within 24 hours of their being filed, and it contains all SEC filings for all corporations required to file, making it a comprehensive source for SEC filing information. EDGAR provides access to its database through subscription only. Its two main subscription options are EDGAR Online Pro (this subscription option costs $100 per month, provides unlimited access to all information, and is designed for institutional investors, investment bankers, auditing and accounting firms, and law firms) and Edgar Online Access (this subscription option costs $19.95 per month, billable quarterly, provides the subscriber with up to 25 search entries per month, and is designed for individual use by private investors, journalists, and students conducting financial research).

EDGAR's database enables the subscriber to define a search by company information, financials, ownership, people, or where the company has appeared in the news.

The Securities and Exchange Commission offers access to all but the most recent EDGAR filings through its web site: http://www.sec.gov/cgi-bin/srch-edgar. This site is free to the user, with its only limitation being that it does not offer information on an up-to-the-minute basis.

The financial statements

It is beyond the scope of this book to present the details contained in financial statements, but you should know that there are three primary — and interrelated — financial reports that every company produces: the statement of cash flow, the income statement and the balance sheet. It's important to understand that financial statements must be read and considered as separate pieces of the puzzle, and must be read with an understanding as to their interrelationships.

When researching a publicly-traded company's financial statements, keep in mind that there are a number of ways for a company to misrepresent its financial position. These include (but are not limited to):

■ Recording revenue too soon. There are three primary ways in which revenue may be recorded too soon: (1) Shipping goods before a sale is finalized. Generally Accepted Accounting Principles (GAAP) require that inventory be shipped out and exchanged for cash or another asset before revenue can be recorded. If revenue is recorded at the time of shipment but before consideration is received, that may be a misrepresentation of the company's financial position. (2) Recording revenue if uncertainties exist. "Uncertainties" in this context refers to there being a likelihood that a buyer will return the goods, or that the buyer might not be able to pay for the goods. An example might be when a company sells products to one of its distributors (at which time the company will record the sale on their balance sheet) only to have those goods returned in the next quarter, after the earnings for the previous quarter have been artificially boosted. A related practice is "channel stuffing," whereby distributors are encouraged to overbuy through the lure of deep discounts. Channel stuffing often results in returned merchandise and reversed sales. (3) Recording revenue when future products or services are still due. This refers to a condition in which revenues are received in anticipation of sales. An example is when a business offers fourth quarter discounts if the customer pays in advance. If delivery is made several weeks or months out, the seller should not record the money received as revenue, but as a liability, because the seller becomes a creditor to the buyer until the product is shipped.

■ Boosting income with one-time gains. This form of accounting manipulation is typically done by selling undervalued assets or by not segregating unusual and nonrecurring gains or losses from recurring income. When income is boosted with one-time gains, revenues are artificially made to appear as if they recur at a rate higher than normal business operations can account for. A company may, in the normal course of business operations, sell non-performing assets (such as a shuttered plant) or business units (such as when Sears Roebuck sold Discover). The accounting manipulation occurs when earnings are presented in such a way as to imply that earnings will continue at that level, when those inside the company know the reality to be quite different. The key to detecting this type of manipulation is to pay particular attention to an earnings report that references the sale of corporate assets, and to then see how those assets are recorded on the balance sheet.

■ Shifting current income or expenses to a later period, or shifting future expenses to the current period. Revenue should be recorded in the period in which it is earned. Shifting income to a future period is typically done to smooth out the cyclical nature of many businesses, which artificially inflates earnings at some future date. Likewise with expenses. By shifting expenses to a later period, the company's managers are making it appear as if their current financial position is stronger than it actually is. The reason executives manipulate expenses and earnings is to present financial reports that show a smooth upward trend. Wide variations of earnings and profits make investors nervous, so CEOs will often "massage the books" to make it appear that their business is being managed in such a way as to produce an expected level of growth. This promotes unfounded investor confidence.

■ Failing to record or disclose all liabilities. "Off-balance-sheet accounting" consists of either minimizing or not disclosing legitimate liabilities. In addition to liabilities that appear on the balance sheet, companies frequently have additional current or pending liabilities (such as lawsuits) that should be disclosed in the footnotes or proxy statements that accompany these financial documents.

Some of these manipulations can be detected by a careful reading of the company's financial reports. However, further investigation is often required. For example, channel stuffing may be detected if it becomes known that employees were asked to post-date sales orders or invoices. The compensation of sales reps may also be a clue. If sales reps receive large commissions for completing sales in a given quarter, they may have incentive to post-date sales transactions. In an instance such as this, a company's executives may not be directly involved in an accounting manipulation, but merely creating the environment for such manipulation to occur.

For a complete explanation of how these accounting gimmicks are perpetrated, and how to spot them, I recommend Howard M. Schilit's book *Financial Shenanigans* (McGraw-Hill). For a full explanation of financial statements from a journalist's perspective, read *Understanding Financial Statements: A Journalist's Guide*, by Jay Taparia (Marion Street Press, Inc.).

Chapter Seven

The Paper Trail: Part II
Researching privately held corporations
and non-profits

Glenn Lewin

Privately held companies and non-profit organizations are often more difficult to research than public companies, but a diligent reporter can still unearth plenty of information.

Privately held corporations

A privately held corporation issues stock, but that stock is generally owned by the officers and employees of the company. Privately held corporations typically raise capital through banks, the Small Business Administration, or venture capitalists. Because a privately held corporation does not issue stock to be traded publicly, it has no obligation to submit 10-K or 10-Q filings with the SEC. Management is, however, legally obliged to submit an annual report (usually to the secretary of state of the state in which it is incorporated). Unlike annual reports of publicly traded corporations, the annual reports of privately held corporations usually contain basic information about the company: the agents and officers of the company, the amount of stock held by each of the company's principals, and any substantial changes (such as a change in its primary business) that occurred over the previous year. The annual reports of publicly traded companies are designed to protect investors; privately held corporations are under no legal obligation to report any of their financial transactions. Additionally, in states where a privately held corporation is required to make an annual filing, these annual filings are not open for public review.

Not all privately held corporations are small. There are a number of privately held corporations that have sales in excess of $1 billion. In some instances these companies are required to submit filings to the SEC (such as when they raise capital through the sale of bonds). As a result, it pays to do an EDGAR search when researching a privately held company. Dun & Bradstreet offers another option when researching a privately held firm. D&B, through its web site www.dnbsearch.com, sells access to its Business Background Reports (the current listed price is $40.55). These reports typically (though not always) contain the following information:

■ Company name and address
■ Parent company name and location
■ Annual sales (estimated)
■ Net worth (estimated)
■ Number of employees
■ A description of the nature of the business
■ Major changes or significant activities, such as bankruptcy filings, changes in ownership, and acquisitions
■ Business history, including incorporation data, par value of shares and ownership information
■ Management background of the principals

The obvious challenge to a business reporter conducting research on a privately held company is not having access to public documents. However, there are a number of avenues open to an enterprising reporter looking for information on privately held companies.

When conducting research on a privately held business, the following are potential sources for documents and document-related information:

Past litigation of the business owner or officers: A pattern of litigation against a company owner, officer or co-owner can serve to provide an insight into both personal and business ethics. If an individual has been engaged in frequent litigation — especially relating to the recoveries of money — that is generally a sign that there is problem in how he is conducting his business.

Workman's compensation claims: Companies engaged in providing either products or services where there is risk (such as chemical plants, meat packing plants/slaughterhouses, or roofing contractors) will tend to have a higher than normal number of workman's comp claims. However, companies that maintain an unsafe work environment will also have a higher than normal number of workman's comp claims, and may reveal something about how the company is managed.

Contractor's liens/lawsuits: A business that has an unusual number of liens or lawsuits against it is a company with a management problem. As an example, when conducting research on a company I was investigating, I learned that both the owner and the corporation had a number of liens against both personal and business assets, and that the owner had a history of business fraud and misconduct. The information learned from this research became part of the story.

Property records (usually found in office of the county clerk where the business is located): Researching property records enables you to "connect the dots" between various individuals in a given community. As an example, when the possibility for a third Chicago-area airport was being debated in the Illinois legislature, and the location for that airport was expected to be in Peotone, Illinois, there were a number of real estate transactions involving Illinois politicians and their relatives (specifically, farmland was being purchased by Illinois politicians and related insiders, with the expectation that it would be resold for a profit). Reporters were able to tell that story by researching property records and real estate transactions.

Incorporation records (these records will reveal who the company's registered agents are, date of incorporation, and location of the business's headquarters): Incorporation records are usually found online through the secretary of state's office in which the business is incorporated. Incorporation records do not offer much in the way of details, but they do enable you to learn the names of company officers. One example of how these records reveal relationships was in the recently reported minority business scandal in Chicago. The City of Chicago operates a minority "set-aside" program in which a certain percentage of the city's business is earmarked for women and minority-owned businesses. However, a number of politically connected insiders were operating front companies in which the listed owner was either a woman or a minority (in one case the mother of a political insider). By researching the incorporation records on file with the state, the reporters were able to identify the owners and officers of these businesses. In Illinois, the following information may be obtained by conducting a Corporation/LLC search: The complete name of the corporation, its status (is it still active, or has it been dissolved), the type of corporation (domestic corporation or limited liability corporation), the date of incorporation, the names and addresses or all agents of the corporation, and who has been added as an agent of the corporation.

OSHA records: OSHA's web site is www.osha.gov. The right hand side of its home page lists a number of links, one of which reads "Statistics," with the sub-category "Inspection Data." Inspection information may be pulled up by SIC or NAIS code, or by state or region. As an example, a search using the criteria of "State: Illinois," "OSHA Office: Chicago North," "Start Date: March 30, 2000," "End Date: March 30, 2005," and "Type of Inspection: Comprehensive" will deliver a list of businesses that have been through OSHA inspections. When you pull up a specific company, you will find the company's name and address, whether or not they are a union shop, a summary of OSHA violations (the number of violations and how serious they have been), and the number and amount of fines OSHA has levied against the business. This can be a valuable resource when researching a company to determine what kind of work environment the company is providing for its clientele (such as a nursing home) or its employees (such as a food processing plant).

EPA and state equivalents: The EPA maintains a web site at www.epa.gov. Its site includes a search engine in which one may enter the name of a business (or a topic, location, etc). For example, a search using the name "Navistar" results in a number of HTML and PDF files in which Navistar's name is contained either in the title or in the text. The first publication found when entering the name "Navistar" is EPA Consent Decree: Navistar International Transportation Corporation Diesel Engines Settlement. The document itself is a 67-page U.S. District Court document detailing the consent decree as a result of the "United States of America vs. Navistar International Transportation Corp." EPA searches may be done by the name of the business, the specific environmental issue of concern, or by geography (e.g., conducting a search by ZIP code, county or state will result in a list of publications and issues affecting the area of interest).

Criminal records (through both current and previous jurisdictions): A criminal records search may result in determining if and when an individual has run afoul of the law. However, one important note of caution: Internet criminal background checks are far from perfect. Therefore, if you find that an individual being researched has a criminal record, it is critical that this information be verified through other sources, such as federal, state or county court or prison records (some, but not all, of these records may be found online). Additionally, if writing about an individual with a criminal record, it is important that the validating information come direct from government sources (such as court or prison records) and not from privately operated data base web sites. This is a protection for the reporter, his or her publication, and for the individual who is the focus of the reporter's research.

Business license records (usually located in the county records office): In most counties the primary purpose of a business license is to have a public record of an individual when that individual is doing business under an assumed name. As an example, "John Samuels Shoe Repair" would not need a "dba certificate" because he is transacting business under his own name (though he would probably need a local business license just to transact business in his community). However, if he were to start transacting business under the name "Smart Step Shoe Repair," he would need a dba certificate. In Illinois that means applying for the license (which is pro forma in almost every situation), and then running three consecutive weekly ads in a local newspaper (approved by the county clerk) announcing that he is transacting business under an assumed name. The information available to a reporter through these records includes the names of all owners of the business, their home address, the date the business was licensed, and the nature of the business itself.

While the Internet is a valuable tool for conducting public document research, one must independently verify any information that would be deemed negative to an individual or company. Public records databases are filled with inaccuracies — records are frequently not updated, and mistakes are made through misspellings, incorrect identification information, and recording errors. Be aware of the limitations associated with using online resources; corroboration is not only a protection for you and your publication, it is the right thing to do.

Researching non-profits

The non-profit sector of the economy accounts for 10 percent to 20 percent of all business activity, depending upon whose estimates are being used. And if that doesn't seem like much, considering that the U.S. economy has a GDP of around $11 trillion, the non-profit sector accounts for anywhere from $1.1 trillion to $2.2 trillion annually. It is also a sector of the economy frequently overlooked by reporters and editors. When you consider that the non-profit sector of the economy includes clubs, charities, social organizations, churches, philanthropic foundations, hospitals, nursing homes, think tanks, museums, zoos, colleges, universities, and privately operated primary and secondary schools (to list but a few), and that it touches every member of society in some manner, it's easy to see just how broad the sector is.

When researching non-profit organizations, a reporter is typically looking to determine:

■ How well managed is the non-profit?

■ What affiliations does this non-profit have with other non-profits? Are there directors that sit on the boards of multiple non-profit organizations? If so, how well managed are those non-profit organizations?

■ Does the non-profit employ relatives or business associates of the director? If so, in what capacity, and how do those hirings affect the financial health of the non-profit?

■ Who is the money going to, and in what percentage? For a charity to retain its non-profit status, many states now require that a minimum percentage of a charity's gross revenue be committed to its stated mission.

■ What is the charity's investment approach? Is it conservative or aggressive? And what impact might either approach have to that charity's ability to fulfill its stated mission?

■ In order for a tax-exempt organization with income over $25,000 to retain its tax-exempt status, it must make an annual Form 990 filing, which details how the money is coming into and and flowing out of the organization. Furthermore, the non-profit is required to make the most recent year's filing available to the public (there is typically a three- to six-month lag time from when the 990 is filed until it becomes available for review).

Charitable organizations often make available a copy of these forms on their web site, while others fulfill the requirement by either mailing out copies or having copies of their 990s available at their headquarters. One Internet resource for obtaining copies of 990s is Guide Star (www.guidestar.org), a national database of charitable organizations. Guide Star is available at no charge, and is accessible simply by signing up and logging in.

Chapter Eight

The Paper Trail: Part III

Databases, libraries and the web

Glenn Lewin

Every business transaction requires a transference of at least some information. Once that information has been transferred (usually from buyer to seller), it is stored, organized and categorized. Much of this information is public, and available through various government agencies. In addition, an unmeasurable amount of information on businesses is available from non-governmental sources, such as private databases and libraries.

In days past, editors gave young reporters assignments that took them to the courthouse or county records office to locate and interpret real estate transactions, court records, and related public documents. It was an important first step in learning what it took to develop background information for stories. And with the digitalization of information (which allows information to be broken up into packets for both storage and retrieval) and the advent of the Internet (which allows that information to be sent to any linked computer), it is now possible for a reporter in Billings, Montana to conduct a records search on data stored in Chicago, New York, Philadelphia or just about anywhere else.

In the past, if a reporter in Chicago was investigating a politician, but that politician had spent most of his life in California, the managing editor had to make a decision: was it worth sending a reporter to California to conduct a public records search? This difficulty of access created a cost vs. return dilemma, a dilemma that — for the most part — no longer exists.

A number of look-up services have been created, offering anyone access to public records from across the country. These services purchase electronic copies of information, organize that information, and allow Internet access, for a fee. The creation of these services has made it possible to conduct complete documents research from a desktop computer. One site I have used extensively is KnowX, a division of ChoicePoint (www.KnowX.com). KnowX purchases and organizes public records and documents and resells them on a "pay as you go" basis. KnowX enables its users to conduct asset searches, bankruptcy searches, business background checks (which is a packaged service containing information on lawsuits, liens, bankruptcies, judgments, and corporate records), and checks to verify if one is holding a professional or business license. There is no cost to open a KnowX account, and searches start at around $10. However, it's important to remember that each search results in a fee, so spending a significant amount of time conducting a search can get expensive.

Government documents

There are three levels of government documents: federal, state and local. All branches of government retain and organize information. There are records of incorporation, driver's licenses, real estate transactions, marriages, births and deaths. The various branches of government compile information for different reasons, so it's important to become familiar with what information is available from each.

Federal government documents include federal court records, patents, federal trademarks, public incorporation filings, and information obtained by various executive branch departments such as Agriculture, Commerce, Transportation, and Justice.

The single best source for accessing this information is the Statistical Abstract of the United States. Published annually by the U.S. Census Bureau, and available through any major book store, this book provides a concise compilation of a variety of statistics, including those describing population, industries, labor, or income distribution (to list but a few). Its research value is that it provides a context in which to understand individual data points. If, for example, you know Honda's total North American sales for 2000, and you are able to use the Statistical Abstract to find the total number of passenger vehicles sold in the U.S. in 2000, you can figure out Honda's share of that market.

Additionally, the federal government employs thousands of experts on a variety of topics, and many are accessible by telephone. Phone numbers to specific government departments may be found in Headquarters USA or Matthew Lesko's Info-Power III, a Guide to Government Resources.

While state government records (and policies for accessing those records) differ from state to state, state government documents typically include records of business incorporation filings, business and professional licensing information, vital statistics (records of births, deaths, marriages, etc.), state criminal and civil court proceedings, tax liens, and department of motor vehicle records.

Local government documents typically include real property ownership records, zoning codes and applications for property rezoning, county and township road expenditures, and new business filings if required at the county or municipal level. The easiest and most common method of accessing local records is at either the county or municipal building. These records are open to anyone willing to spend the time conducting the research. Larger counties have computerized their records and typically offer a number of terminals where research can be conducted. Smaller and more rural counties still maintain physical files (such as Plat survey maps for information on real estate), and those files are accessed through a request to the clerk. In addition to real estate ownership and transactions, counties and municipalities maintain records of births, deaths, and business and marriage licenses. As a business reporter, its important to remember that incorporation records are typically kept on file with the state (usually in the Secretary of State's office, and usually available online), while privately held businesses operating on a "doing business as" basis (i.e., the businesses' owner is operating under an assumed name) need to have a license on file with the county. These licenses require all owners and executives to be named on the license.

Database documents

Encyclopædia Britannica Online defines a database as "any collection of data, or information, that is specially organized for rapid search and retrieval by a computer." Databases are structured to facilitate the storage, retrieval, modification and deletion of data in conjunction with various data-processing operations." Database information is stored and accessed in one of two ways: through direct access (online through the Internet or on-site through a library's internal LAN) or through the licensed purchase of a CD ROM (such as the Harris Selectory listing of U.S manufacturers).

Database information may be stored and retrieved according to a variety of parameters. The Harris Selectory database, for example, allows the user to generate lists of companies by SIC code, type of products manufactured, location, annual sales, number of employees, or by using any combination of these search parameters. Databases accessible via the Internet offer one important advantage over CD ROMs: information in its most current form. EDGAR Online, for example, updates its database daily, as does Standard & Poor's and Dun & Bradstreet. Companies providing public records databases (such as KnowX.com) are typically updated monthly.

In The Reporter's Handbook (St. Martin's Press), Steve Weinberg points out the three general types of databases: superstores, boutiques, and hybrids. Superstore databases, according to Weinberg, "include Dialog, LexisNexis, Dow Jones News/Retrieval, DataStar, NewsNet and DataTimes. These vendors provide access to databases produced by hundreds of organizations." Boutique databases include "database vendors that specialize in providing access to certain types of information: only television news transcripts or driver's records, for example." Hybrids — such as CompuServe, America Online, Genie, Prodigy and Delphi — "provide access to information similar to what is available from superstores, but also offer bulletin boards for communicating with people of like interest."

Online databases charge either by the document downloaded, the time spent conducting a search, a display charge, or the number of items included in a list.

It's important to understand which databases are available, which provide the information you require, and which are affordable. Database documents frequently contain information that, if located and understood, can create new avenues for follow-up investigation.

Libraries and librarians as information resources

There are three types of libraries: public, academic, and special collections. Each serves a different readership. Which library you use depends upon the depth and relevancy of the library's holdings (for example, do not expect to find a complete listing of U.S. Supreme Court citations affecting interstate commerce in a public library), the professionalism of its staff, and the library's access options and policies.

Public libraries are financed by taxpayer dollars, usually through property taxes. A library situated in a suburban community will generally have a broader range of business-related materials in its holdings than will either its rural or urban counterparts.

Academic libraries are funded through endowments and the institutions to which they are attached. State university libraries generally open their doors to any resident of that state, but many will allow only students, faculty, employees and their families check-out privileges. Academic libraries attached to private colleges and universities have similar policies and restrictions.

Special collections libraries usually restrict access to patrons directly associated with the organization or institution to which they are attached. For example, a university law library may restrict access to law school students and professors, while a privately endowed special-collections library may restrict access to approved patrons, such as visiting scholars.

The most knowledgeable and experienced business librarians tend to be employed in either urban or suburban public libraries, or in libraries attached to institutions housing first-rate business schools. A good business librarian is able to quickly direct a researcher to the most appropriate resource. Additionally, business librarians stay on top of changes in the publishing industry and are able to direct researchers to the most accurate and up-to-date resources. Developing relationships with business librarians will save you time and frustration. What takes them minutes to find might easily take you hours.

Don't confine yourself to local libraries. Conduct a library search, and when seeking a library, remember that many offer extensive collections of online information and allow non-residents to purchase out-of-town cards, which gives the patron full access to Internet resources. Take the time to research public library options. You just might find that a library in the next town — or even the next state — will provide you with valuable access to online business resources.

Libraries — especially public libraries — are working to stay relevant in a world where it is increasingly easy to log on and access almost anything. As a result, libraries remain an important information resource for at least the following two reasons:

Libraries are able to purchase and maintain current versions of CD-ROM databases and directories, information resources that are simply too expensive for the average user. And, many publishers license libraries to offer this information online to their patrons (which is why purchasing an out-of-town library card could very well be worth the time, effort and expense).

The ease with which business information may now be stored and retrieved has resulted in an explosion of new list, directory and database publishers. An informed and professional librarian understands how various database publishers obtain their information (an indication of the database's value and relevance), as well as knowing which resources are most appropriate to your specific information requirements.

Organizing the web

The Internet, of course, is packed with resources. Knowing how to organize them is the key to making efficient use of the Web.

My web browser's favorites file contains nine folders, each containing approximately 50 Web site addresses. Of these, there is only a handful I frequent on a regular basis, but they deliver more than 85 percent of the online documents I use for background research when writing articles and reports.

Because the Internet is so large and ubiquitous, it is impossible to bookmark every possible Web address you might use in conducting documents research. Additionally, it is a constantly changing and evolving entity, so any extended list of sites will soon become obsolete. Therefore, the following is a listing of *topics* relevant to conducting primary and secondary document research, along with search engine keywords needed to locate specific Web sites:

Business newspapers, magazines and journals

Of limited direct research value, these sites offer business news and information. Examples include the online editions of The Wall Street Journal, Barron's Online, Bloomberg.com, Business Week Online, Fortune.com, and Forbes.com. Keywords for locating sites: Business News / Business Newspapers / Business Magazines / Business Journals.

Case studies online
Managed and operated by major business schools (Harvard, Wharton, University of Chicago, etc.) and consulting firms (such as McKinsey & Company), these sites provide access on both a no-charge and fee basis. Direct research value is limited, as archival research is often not possible, but they do offer insight into topics of current interest within the major business schools. Keywords for locating sites: Business Case Studies Online.

Business research assistance
These sites offer links to other sites which provide specific business, market and industry information. Many of these sites are operated and managed by public and university libraries. Pay particular attention to any site specifically designed to assist business journalists (such as Power Reporting and the site operated by Investigative Reporters and Editors, Inc.). Keywords for locating sites: Business Research / Business Research Online / Business Journalism / Advocacy Journalism / Advocacy Business Research / Business Database Information.

Business directories & related business information
These sites aid in locating business names, addresses, stock symbols, annual sales, number of employees, etc. Preferred sites include Dow Jones Interactive, Thomas Register, Info USA, CorpTech, and Dun & Bradstreet. Keywords for locating sites: Business Directories Online / Business Information / Business Articles Online.

Stocks & stock market information
Of value when researching stock prices or general market information, these sites provide stock symbols, pricing information and general market information. Keywords for locating sites: Stock Market Information / Stock Prices / Stock Analysis / Stock Exchanges.

SEC filings & annual report services
The two primary sites for retrieving and downloading SEC filing information are EDGAR Online and 10K-Wizard. Annual report sites link the user to a company's annual report page (usually downloadable through Adobe Acrobat). The EDGAR Online and 10K-Wizard

sites are recommended because both offer filings as they appear to the SEC. Keywords for locating sites: SEC / SEC Filings / Annual Reports / Annual Reports Online.

Statistical & demographic information

Statistical information includes compiled data such as the gross national product, leading economic indicators, or total product output by industry. Statistical information enables the researcher to compare the specific (one company's annual sales) with the general (total industry sales). Keywords for locating sites: Statistics / Statistical Abstracts / Demographics / Statistical and Demographic Information.

Association locators

Industry and trade associations can be excellent resources for business reporters. Industry associations are in business to serve member companies with news and information affecting their industry, through federal and state lobbying efforts, and by offering education and training for employees of member companies. Keywords for locating sites: Associations / Industry Associations / Trade Associations / Professional Associations / Societies, or the industry name in which you are conducting research followed by the word Association (as in Chemical Manufacturer's Association or Industrial Glass Manufacturer's Association).

Information on international commerce & trade

The World Wide Web has a number of sites offering information on international commerce, export trade, foreign companies, or foreign markets. Keywords for locating sites: International Trade / International Commerce / International Economics / World Trade / Foreign Trade / World Economic Output.

Chapter Nine

Finding and Developing Sources

Glenn Lewin

Experienced reporters develop and rely upon sources, i.e., people within their beat who supply information and help advance stories. Business reporting is no different. But who are these sources? Where might they be found? How can they be developed? And how can one verify the quality and veracity of the information they provide?

Different sources for different business beats

The highest profile business journalists write for publications with a national reach, such as The Wall Street Journal, Forbes, Fortune, Business Week, etc. However, most business journalism is being done at smaller, regional publications, such as the Rockford Register Star, the Charlotte Business Journal, or the Sherman, Texas Herald Democrat. Publications such as these typically have circulations under 100,000, and their business desks often consist of one or two editors/reporters.

The type of sources one develops will depend upon the manner in which business is being covered. In the larger, national publications, reporters tend to specialize by industry, whereas journalists writing for local or regional newspapers or magazines tend to be generalists, and their beats tend to be defined by geography rather than industry.

Finding business sources locally

The business editors of local and regional publications typically have one or two major employers for whom labor news (such as plant layoffs or union contract votes) is covered on a regular basis. Additionally, these more localized publications also cover county or regional business development issues, chamber-of-commerce related issues, the impact of larger businesses on smaller businesses (such as how the opening of a new Wal-Mart is likely to affect existing retailers), real-estate related issues, and how changes in state taxes are likely to impact local employers. Business reporters for these publications tend to be generalists, and their focus is almost entirely local. As a result, sources are developed locally, and from a diverse number of industries and companies.

In looking to develop worthwhile sources, the first questions the reporter might ask herself are, "Where is the bulk of my reporting likely to take place? What sources will I need so that I am able to consistently develop reliable information?" If, for example, that reporter is responsible for covering the labor issues of a multi-national manufacturer with a plant employing 1,500 people, her readers will be interested in any news involving layoffs, work stoppages, strikes, or the outsourcing of work. In this example, the reporter will want to develop a relationship with the plant's public relations or press office, as well as with the plant manager and assistant plant manager. However, there are a number of other sources that this reporter might look to develop. These would include local union leadership, plant personnel (both exempt and hourly employees), and — if at all possible — plant suppliers and delivery people who frequent the plant and are in a position to observe and speak with plant personnel.

The reporter's objective is to provide as complete and honest a picture as is possible with the information she has developed. Therefore, each source will provide a different perspective, and the compilation of these various perspectives should lead to a more complete understanding of any issue. For example, the plant's press relations office will provide the company's side of any issue; the plant manager will provide the perspective of local management; union leadership will provide the perspective of how a specific issue will affect its members; and plant personnel will provide the perspective of how a given issue will impact the individual. And finally, an outsider's perspective may be obtained by interviewing those supplying goods and services to the plant. In this example, it's important to note that each of these various sources will not only have a different perspective on any given issue, but they will also provide varying aspects of information that will, when pieced together, provide the reader with a more complete understanding of the story.

Let's now look at other sources one might develop locally, by area of interest to the reader.

Business development issues

New business development is often spearheaded by elected officials (city or county), real estate developers, and the local chamber of commerce.

One example of this blending of business and government is Rockford Illinois' Council of 100, a business development organization that has worked "hand in glove" with local government officials to stimulate growth in both Rockford and Winnebago County. One major success was to expand Rockford Airport runways to accommodate larger aircraft. This resulted in UPS moving its Midwestern hub from Chicago's O'Hare Airport to Rockford.

Chamber of commerce issues

Issues important to a local chamber of commerce include the impact of local sales taxes, real estate taxes, taxes aimed at specific products (alcohol, liquor) or services (hotels, recreational activities), laws affecting employment, (such as a local — and substantially higher — minimum wage recently passed by the City of Madison, Wisconsin), or zoning. Sources for advancing stories on these issues include prominent chamber members and the attorneys responsible for either drafting or challenging taxation affecting local industry.

The impact of larger businesses on smaller businesses

This is becoming known as the Wal-Martization of America, but Wal-Mart is not the only major corporation using its financial advantage to muscle smaller competitors. As most of these battles are now occurring in rural America, local business reporters are often those closest to the issue and in the best position to report on it. Ongoing sources relating to this issue might be found in the economics department of a major university (because many university professors have conducted impact studies on what happens to the fabric of a community when one major retailer replaces a number of smaller retailers), or stock analysts responsible for tracking companies such as Wal-Mart. [Note: it is important to try to obtain quotes from spokespeople for companies such as Wal-Mart or Target, but regarding this specific issue, they will frequently issue a "no comment."]

A recent example of this issue has been occurring in Wisconsin, where Wal-Mart has been opening a number of "super stores" (i.e., they sell food in addition to discount merchandise). Reporters looking to describe the impact on local economies have interviewed economics professors at both the University of Wisconsin and Marquette University. Their expertise and insight have helped the average reader to understand the impact "big box" retailers have on rural economies.

Local real estate issues

A typical real-estate issue of interest to readers is how ex-urban sprawl is changing the demographics of a community. Another real estate-related issue which has arisen in recent years is how local governments have been condemning residential property, forcing homeowners to sell that property to the government. The government then re-zones the property as commercial, and auctions it off to the highest commercial bidder. This is being done on the theory that more taxes are realized from commercial property than from residential property, and as a result it is in the "public interest." The U.S. Supreme Court recently made headlines when it ruled that the city of New London, Connecticut can condemn property in the interest of promoting economic development.

But there are a number of other issues related to real estate that are of interest to the readers of the business pages of local newspapers. One recent example comes from suburban Milwaukee, where a real estate developer was willing to build, at no charge, a new school for the local district. The "catch" was that the local district would have to move the school and sell the property on which the existing school was located to that developer for fair market value. The developer owned property adjacent to where the school is currently located; by combining the two parcels of land the developer would realize a far greater profit than the cost of the new school. The issue for the community was safety for the students. The proposed new school location was to be in a high-traffic zone, and many students would have to cross a major highway when walking to class. Sources for stories such as these include local community leaders, real estate developers, elected officials, and residents directly affected by changes to existing zoning

Finding business sources within a specific industry

Reporters covering business on a national level tend to focus on specific industries or sectors within the economy. Reporters for national publications typically cover areas such as the "tech sector," the "transportation sector," or the" telecommunications industry." Unlike their brethren writing for a local or regional readership, reporters writing for national publications tend to think in terms of what national or even international impact an event might have. Examples include the collapse of Enron and its impact on former employees, stockholders and creditors; the impact that outsourcing (and in-sourcing) is having on the U.S. economy; the strength or weakness of the U.S. dollar and its effect on U.S. companies; or how the price of crude on world markets affects the airline industry.

In each of these examples, reporters rely on a variety of sources, The following is a list of possible sources a reporter might use when covering an industry or sector of the economy.

■ Executive managers of industry-leading companies: These people are frequently hard to reach, but in every industry some executives are media-savvy and willing to talk.

■ Industry consultants: Consultants exist in every industry, and are frequently able to offer a "big picture" view of what is occurring within their industry. Consultants usually have industry management experience, but many will speak only on condition of anonymity.

■ Industry analysts: Brokerage houses and large research firms employ industry analysts. As an example, Bob Goodman, a Senior Analyst for the Yankee Group, is an industry expert quoted on stories relating to the high-tech industry sector.

■ Economists: Both university and private industry economists are oft-cited sources for stories relating to issues impacting consumers and the economy.

■ Trade magazine editors and writers: Nearly every industry has at least one (and often several) trade magazines supporting it. Articles typically revolve around innovations, trends and challenges facing companies within the industry. As a result, writers and editors of these publications have a myriad of their own contacts and sources they may be willing to share. A listing of trade publications may be found in The Directory of Business Information Resources, which is published by Grey House Publishing, Lakeville, Connecticut.

■ Executive recruiters: Executive search firms often specialize in one, two or a few industries. Because of the service they provide, they are privy to a great deal of inside industry information. But remember, as with industry consultants, their income is derived from the services they provide to their industry, so they are likely to speak only on the condition of anonymity.

■ Sales reps: It is my experience that some of the best sources within an industry are its sales reps. Their job is to disseminate information to customers for the purpose of promoting their company's products or services. Gaining access to a sales rep is far easier than gaining access to an executive.

Developing ongoing business sources

Once a reporter learns who has what information, and how information advances stories, the next step is to develop ongoing sources. The reason is self-evident: if a reporter is writing about either a region (local) or an industry (national), stories relating to certain issues will appear time and again. Developing ongoing sources is vital to a reporter's effectiveness.

In developing a source, it is a good idea to keep in mind that the reporter-source relationship is both business and professional in nature; it is not a friendship. While reporters develop sources because it helps them advance their stories, sources provide information to reporters for reasons of their own. Sometimes a source may be in it for the free publicity obtained by being quoted. Sometimes a source may be looking to do the right thing, or on the other side of the coin, to get back at an employer or former employer. There are as many reasons sources will talk to reporters as there are sources. It is up to the reporter to exercise judgment and professionalism as to when, why and how a source is used.

The process of developing an ongoing source is not complicated, but it does take time, effort and tact. And it is not a one-way street; a reporter has to be willing to give in order to receive. When developing a source, a reporter's best friend is his or her personality. Respect, consideration and a smile go a long way towards getting someone to open up. It's important to find common ground and to build bridges from that common ground. And once someone has opened up and is willing to talk, it is incumbent upon the reporter to keep in contact from time to time — even if there is no current story for which the reporter needs information. Nothing will turn off a person more than if they feel used. "Touch base" calls are important, especially if the reporter has some tidbit of information he or she is willing to share with the source.

Consider the following: a reporter has developed a relationship with a local business leader who has, from time to time, provided the reporter a substantial amount of background information on issues relating to local business development. In one instance background information provided to the business reporter by this business leader enabled the reporter to tell an important story of significant local interest. Now, a few months later, the reporter calls the business leader and shares a piece of information that is of interest to this business leader. So long as the reporter is not compromising another source or his/her own ethics, this "give and take" helps to solidify the relationship and will, in all probability, result in even more information in the future.

The art of developing sources is nothing more than the art of building relationships. But for a reporter, the trick is in knowing who is worth developing (based on what information they are able to provide), and how best to maintain those relationships (i.e., being friendly without becoming too familiar). And as a reporter progresses in her career, a good reporter will learn that time spent in developing the right sources will return substantial dividends.

Chapter Ten

Writing Business News

Robert Reed

Some journalists are natural reporters who love the thrill of the chase and have a knack for finding the right information at the right time. Other journalists are born writers who can take the most mundane facts and turn them into enviable prose. The best journalists, in my opinion, are those who can blend these talents and create business stories that are deeply researched, well sourced and a pleasure to read —and do it all on deadline. Throughout this book, we've outlined methods to improve your reporting and offered advice on ways to get deeper into the substance of complicated issues and events. Now, here are some guidelines for anticipating and producing urgent, cutting-edge business reporting and writing.

Develop a point of view

There are more sources for news out there than ever before and a great many people (especially young adults) won't go to a newspaper if they believe the stories are a mere rehash of what they've already read online or seen elsewhere.

As we've pointed out, one way to stay in the game is by breaking news. Local newspapers have the built-in advantage of knowing their community better than anyone else, so use those contacts and connections.

That said, local business reporting has to be interpretive and analytical if it is going to create and add value for the reader. "Interpretive and analytical" are not code words for biased and one-sided, nor is it permission to just go out and write whatever you feel like. It is however, license—for lack of a better word—to make a honest effort at getting to the essence and truth of a situation.

To do that, stories profit from a point-of-view. Let's say, for example, the hometown airline is having financial trouble. Industry experts and market sources tell you the only way it can save itself is by filing bankruptcy or selling off most of its assets. Is it fair to make that the main angle and point of view of your story? You bet. Rest assured that a beleaguered airline won't agree with you and chances are it may even give a statement to the contrary, saying all is well.

But when diligent reporting, asking the right questions of the right sources, and having the facts all lead to an honest conclusion, then you have an obligation to tell readers what that conclusion is and what it may mean to them. In short, good business reporting is not about taking dictation (from a company or any source) and going with only that limited viewpoint. It's about digging and vetting information (on deadline) and reaching important conclusions that will not only tell today's story but tee-up the other stories that will assuredly follow.

Road trip

Really good business stories tend to unfold over time. It's almost like they have an arc to them. The best of all worlds is to break the story and then stay a step ahead of the competition by breaking news on every major turn of events in the story. Be prepared. When a major story breaks, take a little time to brainstorm with sources about where it's going to lead and develop a "road map" (mental or real notes) about the likely path the news will take. Word of caution: Don't be so wed to this map that you fail to recognize a change of events or important detours in coverage. This is just a way of anticipating, not merely reacting, to big unfolding stories.

Let's take the aforementioned troubled airline as an example. For argument's sake, we'll assume you already know that the carrier is coping with some huge troubles. Passenger loads are low, fuel costs are up, lenders are unhappy, and unionized workers are being forced to take pay cuts. The company is burning cash. One more thing — officially management is "in the bunker," meaning it won't talk to the press on the record.

Downsize jargon!

Corporate America has cornered the market on business jargon. It's a journalist's job to cut through this clutter and report what's really going on. Here's a few examples of corporate-speak that should not go unchallenged.

Right-sizing or **re-engineering**. That means the company is going to fire a lot of people.

Synergy. That means the company is going to fire a lot of people.

Facetime (as in "The three hour drive from Springfield to St. Louis gave the sales manager and his rep some quality facetime")

Thinking outside the box. Current management hasn't a clue how to fix its problems.

Win-win. There's no such thing. There's upside and downside to every deal and situation.

30,000 foot view (as in "A few years ago two Detroit newspaper writers authored a book on the Daimler-Chrysler merger; it offered a 30,000 foot view of the merger").

Low-hanging fruit. The easy decisions have been made. Now it's on to the hard part.

Sounds daunting? Not really. What you have here is the making of some great coverage.

Under such circumstances you can anticipate only a few scenarios: The company files for bankruptcy reorganization to work out a deal in court with lenders, unions, and other creditors; the airline goes crawling to its lenders (or huge vendors like engine makers and jet lease providers) and begs for new, more manageable financing terms; or it sells or "merges" with another airline or company (less likely because the buyer would have to take on a lot of those liabilities).

First, try to determine the most plausible strategy. In this case, it's probably bankruptcy. You can wait until the carrier files (and then everyone's on the story) or you can write a "curtain-raiser" that will outline all its troubles and why bankruptcy is the likely move.

Once the airline has filed (and all hell has busted loose), you need to anticipate what the filing will mean to the company and its stakeholders. Don't just report assets and liabilities and leave it at that. Bankruptcy court proceedings (and related documents) are public records and a treasure trove of information.

Go into the bankruptcy asking some important questions: Where's the drama? What's going to stay? What's going to go? Will union workers be asked to give up some pay and benefits? Will pension and health care plans be trimmed? Will current top management remain? What type of fees will be generated by the bankruptcy lawyers (who get paid before everyone)?. Who will lend the company money DIP financing (for debtor-in-possession) while the airline wings through the court proceedings?

Also, what's the timetable? How long will it take? What's the game plan for emerging out of bankruptcy? What will this company become? How will it look and function?

Just considering these questions can help you build a framework that can make for better stories and overall great coverage.

True, there will be times when it all becomes too technical or gets bogged down. And you're not there to chart every hiccup. Keep perspective. Remember, the trick is to know when major turns in the coverage road will occur. Every great story has such turning points and your role is to anticipate and cover them like a seasoned pro, even if this is all new to you.

Value-added. This is when a company is selling the same product as competitors but attaches a couple of new, often unneeded services or devices, and then charges more.

24/7. Yes, some global companies and the government work all the time. But human beings don't and when they say they are "on the job 24/7," it's nonsense.

Incentivize (as in "The sales staff was incentivized to sell only whole life insurance").

Core competency. Does this infer that anything the company does outside its main business center is incompetent?

Disintermediation. A fancy term for cutting out the middle man. It's often used to describe Internet companies that deal directly with consumers.

Transparency. This one pops up when a company is under pressure to be clear and open about what its doing. In other words, "not Enron."

Efforting "He is efforting to get the work out before tomorrow's deadline."

— Reed and Lewin

Write and edit like you mean it

The potential for great business stories is often hurt by weak writing. Even the best reporting can get lost if a story isn't crafted properly. That's why it's so important to write stories with urgency and a sense of mission. Here are some tips on crafting a story that will resonate with readers:

Writing a lead. First and foremost, make it accessible. Go over your reporting and pick out the most important news or theme. Once you've decided on the angle, take a brief step back and think about how you would tell this story to a friend. Would you say "profits were up 23 percent and the company is feeling positive about its annual sales?" Unlikely. Chances are you'd say, "The company is turning the corner" and then bring up the earnings figures later. In other words, don't hit the reader with numbers right away — give them a little guidance before springing data on them.

National stories go local

On any given day, a national story breaks or a trend emerges that affects nearly everyone. The tendency is to let the national press have its day and tell these tales. But local media can also weigh in on these trends stories. Some examples:

■ Economic data. Interest rates, unemployment numbers, consumer confidence or gross national product are just a few examples. After all, by definition, a hike or decline in a bellwether interest rate will assuredly be felt by anyone who has a variable mortgage, credit card, auto loan or interest-bearing account. A rise or fall in the jobless rate gives a newspaper the opportunity to view its area's employment scene. In short, use national economic trends as a means of connecting with local readers.

■ Energy costs. The flux in energy prices has a direct impact on the cost of goods, consumer spending habits and investing. Let the national press cover OPEC, but bring the story home to your local readers by gauging what energy costs will mean to their commercial and personal lives.

■ Stock market swings. There's no shortage of stock watchers and players. And the national and online media do a pretty good job of covering the horse race. But local press should have a couple of resident stock experts on hand to help report the importance of the market's mood swings and to give readers some idea of the investment environment.

Here's an example every business writer faces: As regulators compel companies to be more open and candid about their finances, many publicly traded corporations now issue earnings "guidance" reports a few weeks before revealing their actual quarterly results. These statements are closely monitored by investors and traders.

In this example, Company XYZ, a global manufacturer based in your hometown, announces earnings will fall short of industry analyst forecasts by at least 10 percent. The company notes it will take a one-time charge to earnings to pay for ending a long-standing class action lawsuit against it, which will result in a multi-million dollar settlement with the plaintiffs. The company had vowed to fight the lawsuit. Following its announcement, the company's stock price goes up 10 percent to $52.34 a share — a new 52-week high — amid heavy trading volume.

Based on these spare facts, what's the most compelling lead? First thing you do is decide the newest and best angle. For example:

■ If the settlement was expected and the market reaction is the most compelling angle:

> Company XYZ's stock price skyrocketed today as investors cheered a proposed settlement of a long-standing legal dispute. Shares zoomed 10 percent in heavy trading to $52.34, a new 52-week high for XYZ, which has seen its share price drop because of the class action lawsuit's potential fallout and growing Wall Street anxiety over its financial impact on the company.

■ If the settlement was unexpected then that's the news and the stock angle is secondary:

> Giving up its tenacious battle to beat opponents in a long-running class action lawsuit, Company XYZ today agreed to a multi-million dollar settlement that will gut its quarterly corporate earnings by up to 10 percent. Still, word of the settlement gave investors hope of brighter days ahead and boosted the company's stock price by 10 percent to $52.34 a share in heavy trading.

Foreshadowing facts. No one says a lead has to be just one paragraph. Many times, business stories are multi-dimensional. In that case, think of your lead as being one to four paragraphs. Use those paragraphs to foreshadow the major elements of a story.

An example: A local company is losing money and is under siege from various stakeholders and its hometown is worried about layoffs and cutbacks.

The structure of your lead may be four interlocking paragraphs that telegraph what this story may encompass these key elements:

Company X lost a lot of money.

Top management is under fire from shareholders.

Management is fighting back.

Local residents are worried about layoffs and factory closures.

Perhaps you follow up the fourth paragraph with a strong quote from the right source (to give the story more personality) and then get into the guts of the writing. The trick here is to use the top of the story as your map to the rest of the story. Once the top is organized you can then write in sections — weaving in your reporting and analysis — and transition to each section with a well-turned phrase or quote. You'd be surprised how this approach helps the readers follow complicated stories from beginning to end.

Here's an example of a multi-paragraph lead using foreshadowing to signal the main points this business feature will touch upon. It tells the readers right at the beginning what to expect in this article. It seeks to connect with everyday readers by using pop culture references, while at the same time presenting the more serious premise. The topic of this article is that MBAs are to blame for Corporate America's problems. The lead illustrates the MBAs' fall from grace (to hook the reader); states what they are being blamed for (the premise of the article); and discusses the great debate it has launched in academic and corporate circles (signaling this is a hot topic with many dimensions and nuances.) This article of 2,000 words appeared in the November 2004 issue of Chicago magazine:

Dwindling Profits
By Robert Reed
Reprinted with permission of Chicago magazine

Once lionized as a high priest of business, the possessor of an MBA has become a punch line. Here's an example: A television ad for Federal Express shows a young employee being asked by a supervisor to ship some packages. With a tinge of condescension, the worker notes he has an MBA, prompting his boss to respond: "In that case, I'll have to show you how to do it."

Elsewhere, these onetime cultural heroes are being promoted as cutthroat, backstabbing, vile capitalist tools — witness the hype for the second season of NBC's hit show The Apprentice. Four of the original 18 candidates vying to learn from Donald Trump are "armed with an MBA," as the network puts it, and each is more obnoxious than the last.

In fact, the turnaround in perception is more than just an entertainment note. Fairly or not, businesspeople with a master's degree in business administration — in common parlance, they've been equated with their credential and are now universally known as MBAs, just as doctors are labeled MDs — are being blamed for the many ills that have plagued business recently. Corporate scandals, excessive executive compensation, outsourcing of jobs, and the dismantling of companies are increasingly linked to the cold and calculating MBA mindset.

The perception has prompted a vocal debate within business and academic circles about the "MBA types," and even some soul-searching at the places that churn thousands of them out annually — the nation's elite MBA programs, including Northwestern University's Kellogg School of Management and the University of Chicago Graduate School of Business. And the backlash comes at a time when even those graduating with degrees from leading schools are scrambling for work.

"In the 1990s, there was an idealized view that MBAs were great and wonderful. Now they're not thought of that way," says James Waldroop, who until 2001 helped develop MBA programs for Harvard Business School and is a co-developer of CareerLeader.com, an online career assessment program.

Robert Magee, senior associate dean of faculty and research at Kellogg, points out that the blend of a difficult economic climate and the notorious ethical lapses that spawned the era of Enron whets the public's appetite to lay blame. "In that milieu, the MBA is kind of a convenient target," he says.

This is long for a lead, but it captures the readers' attention and tells them what to expect. The rest of the article develops the ideas introduced here.

Look lively. I'd like to have a dime for every executive profile that began by describing the executive's office. Borrrrrrring. Look for color even in what appears to be the most color-less story. Push your story subjects for anecdotes and examples. Delve into the personal lives, hobbies and activities of the people you cover. Talk to them about their lives! You never know when something great might pop up that can be used to give texture and color to your story. But if you don't ask, you'll never find it.

Quotes aren't just for stock bids. One of the best ways to get great quotes is to engage more with your subject. Don't just rush in and get down to business. For instance, even though a CEO's schedule is tight, many will still take time to talk about matters other than business. A comment about society, sports or the arts may shed as much light on an interviewer as what they say about their company or business situation. Keep your ears open for these pearls and use them in your stories.

Get down and dirty. When covering a company, don't just go to its gleaming headquarters and stop there. Make the effort to see its factories, outposts and major offices. In doing so, you'll get a sense of the company's culture and mission. As important, it will give you fodder for many stories and greater understanding of how the company fits into its industry and society. If it's a global concern, tap into some overseas sources, like newspapers or community activists, to see how the company operates in the provinces and how it's regarded. Also, you may find that managers who are posted overseas have more autonomy and can be more open with the press than executives who are stateside and under the careful eye of their bosses. It's worth a try.

Most of all, tell a story. Write with confidence! Cut down on weasel words like "may," "could," "possibly," "appears," or "is expected." These words are crutches. Good reporting can help erase such tentative terms. Remember, the more self-assured you are in your reporting and editing skills the easier it is to write a compelling narrative. And that is the goal — to tell a story in the clearest, strongest voice you can muster.

Chapter Eleven

Numbers and Statistics

Glenn Lewin

The purpose of this chapter is not to attempt to teach you mathematics, but to provide you with an awareness of key topics and ideas relating to numbers and statistics. The objective is to give you the ammunition necessary to perform the essentials of the job, which is to ask intelligent questions and to accurately report what you have learned.

Mathematics, and to a lesser extent statistics, is the language of business. While business leaders may speak fondly of a "corporate mission," in the final analysis it's the numbers that govern their decisions. It is for this reason that business reporters are often at a disadvantage when interviewing business executives, many of whom spend much of their time compiling, analyzing and interpreting the numbers that most affect their bottom line. Additionally, mathematics has its own language and symbology that intimidates those unfamiliar with it.

Familiarity with numbers and statistics

As a business reporter, the objective is to develop a number awareness. Numbers rule business, and since that is our beat, we need to be able to cope with them.

As a business reporter with an undergraduate degree in English Literature and almost no training in math, I worked to develop an attitude about math and statistics that encompasses the following:

■ A lack of formal education in math or statistics need not keep one from asking questions. In fact, much can be learned if one is willing to dive into the numbers and work to understand their context and meaning.

■ Statistics as a discipline encompasses two general fields: descriptive statistics and inferential statistics. Descriptive statistics are what we use when discussing baseball batting averages, the stock market, or business cycles. Descriptive statistics are used to analyze data and describe trends. Pie charts, bar charts, or pictographs are all graphical representations of descriptive data. Inferential statistics is when a representative sample is taken, tested, and used to draw conclusions about a population based on a small (but representative) sampling of that population. Examples of inferential statistics include public opinion polling, or survey research used to determine customer attitudes about products or services.

■ It is dangerous to accept statistical research at face value. Almost all statistical research is sponsored and has an agenda. As an example, when Pepsi conducted its "Pepsi Challenge" taste test years ago, they trumpeted the fact that a majority of those tested preferred Pepsi over Coke. However, when the testing protocols were closely examined, it became obvious that the test conditions used were designed for an outcome favorable to Pepsi. This lack of independence in statistical research is perceived as being so bad that in her book *Tainted Truth: The Manipulation of Fact in America*, Cynthia Crossen writes "the commercialization of research means that the number of independent voices is dwindling. Every university professor, researcher or doctor who sells his soul to self-interested sponsors comforts himself with the same rationale: 'I can accept this money without compromising my independence; my ethics are intact; I won't be biased.' But it is never so."

■ Statistics carry with them the imprimatur of being an objective avenue to the truth. This is their strength, as well as their contribution to the advancement of knowledge. But it is also why it statistics are so readily misused and abused. Whether it is a group of scientists making the case for global warming, or the National Manufacturers Association arguing in favor of tort reform, their arguments are statistical in nature. In a sense, they are saying "you should believe us because we have arrived at this conclusion through objective research." Sometimes that is true, but often it is not.

■ Statistics are used throughout the business environment. Statistics are used to manage quality (such as with statistical process control protocols, or through the implementation of a Six Sigma program), assess risk, determine prices, or decide which customers are and are not worth pursuing.

■ Data mining and data manipulation are two major applications of statistics in the modern business environment. Example: the insurance industry has discovered that there is a statistical correlation between bad credit and claims on homeowners' insurance policies. As a result, some insurance carriers have started pulling credit reports on new policy applicants. Example: department stores have discovered that if a customer returns items a certain number of times

Why numbers matter

When discussing numbers and statistics with reporters, I frequently ask the following questions:

■ What is the approximate population of Mexico? (104 million people, the 11th most populated country in the world)

■ What are the world's three most populated cities? (Tokyo, with 34 million people; Mexico City, with 18 million people, and New York City, with 17 million people)

■ What is the population of Canada? (approximately 32 million people)

■ What is the population of the U.S.? (approximately 293 million people, the world's third most populated country, behind China and India)

■ What was the U.S. budget deficit for 2004? (approximately $400 billion, fiscal year 2004)

■ What is the total debt for the United States? (approximately $7.7 trillion, January 2005)

■ What is the total Gross Domestic Product for the U.S.? ($11 trillion, 2003)

■ What is the current U.S. trade deficit? ($58.3 billion as of January, 2005)

■ Which U.S. corporation had the most revenues in 2003? (Wal-Mart, at $253 billion) What U.S. corporation was number two? (ExxonMobil, at $213 billion)

Think of the above examples. Why is it important to know the populations of Mexico, Canada, or even the U.S., for that matter? Because, throughout much of history demographics have played a major role on world events. In the center of North America lies the United States. We are the world's largest economy with the world's third largest popula-

throughout the year, they cease being profitable to the retailer. As a result, certain retailers now have unpublished policies as to how many times they will allow a customer to return merchandise throughout the course of a year. Example: for the past several years airlines have utilized a dynamic pricing policy, whereby the price of a ticket varies not only by whether it is a coach, business or first class seat, but also by when it was purchased. The earlier a seat is purchased, the less expensive it is...unless the seat remains unsold. Then, like milk that is about to spoil, the airline sells the ticket at a bargain price to ensure the plane flies full.

tion. To our north is Canada, with a population a little over one-tenth of the U.S., but with an economy much like our own (though substantially smaller, of course). Canada is a stable neighbor. To our south is Mexico. Mexico is the world's 11th most populated country, has the world's second most populated city, but with an economy unable to support its population. In fact, for all practical purposes, Mexico is a third world country, with much of its infrastructure in disrepair or nearly non-existent. As a result, each year between one million and three million Mexican citizens cross the border illegally in search of a better life. This population influx is beginning to have significant ramifications for our politics, our culture, and even how we view ourselves as Americans. An awareness of the size of our respective populations helps us to understand why events are unfolding as they are.

Continuing with the above examples, many people (including business reporters) confuse the budget deficit with the national debt. The deficit is how far short revenues fall below spending this year, while the national debt is the total amount of money owed treasury bond holders. The national debt is the accumulation of all those years of deficits. Having a basic understanding of these numbers puts them in context. If the national debt is $7.7 trillion dollars and growing, and the gross domestic product is $11 trillion, as a nation we are approaching a point where the total debt will exceed the total amount of goods and services we produce in a year. This (according to some economists) could cause the major purchasers of our treasury notes to lose confidence and invest in foreign stocks, bonds and currencies. Were that to happen, it would drive up the interest rates paid to treasury bond investors because our government would have to compete more aggressively for investors dollars. This, in turn, would accelerate our national debt.

Asking the right questions

As both a business writer and reporter, I have often been presented with arguments that are based on mathematics, statistics or both. This experience has helped me to formulate a series of questions I use whenever I review quantitative information:

■ Who is sponsoring or paying for the research? What agenda (open or hidden) do they have?

■ If an argument is made based on survey research, may I have access to the questionnaire used to conduct the research? How objective or unbiased are the questions?

■ Was the sampling truly random? As an example, market research based on focus groups is very often biased towards a middle-class, young white population because that is very often the target market. However, problems arise when the users of that research imply or state directly that this demographic speaks for the population as a whole.

■ Are supporting charts or graphs representative of the data? Understand that charts and graphs are visual representations of quantitative data, and as a result are subject to subtle — and sometimes not so subtle — manipulation.

■ Do the numbers really support the conclusions? Remember that correlation does not equal causation. This is a fundamental statistical concept, and an important one to keep in mind. Just because two events are linked by a strong linear correlation does not mean that one event causes the other. For example, there is a statistical correlation between who wins the Super Bowl (the AFC or NFC representative) and how well the stock market performs throughout the rest of the year. If the NFC representative wins, the stock market tends to have an up year, but when the AFC representative wins, the market tends to be down for the year. This is a coincidence or statistical anomaly, not a correlation. Life is filled with examples where correlation does not equal causation.

■ If an average is quoted, is it an accurate representation of the data? Each data set has three averages, the mean (which is the arithmetic average), the median (which is the number that falls into the middle of an organized set of data) and the mode (which is the most frequently occurring number). When quoting average levels of income, housing prices, prices of new cars — as examples — it is better to use the median number, as the mean is more affected by numbers at the extreme. For example, if you are quoting the salaries of 20 randomly selected individuals and one of those individuals is Bill Gates, his income will greatly skew the other 19 incomes toward the high side, which means that the data are not truly representative of the sample. However, Gates' income will not affect the distribution nearly as much if that distribution is represented by the median income level.

■ Are the numbers being quoted raw numbers or percentages? The following is a true statement: "The more than three thousand people killed in the World Trade Center attacks was the largest single loss of life against Americans from a foreign force." While true, the 1,500 or so people killed in the Pearl Harbor attack represented a larger percentage of Americans because the U.S. population as a whole was substantially smaller (approximately 100 million people in 1941, as opposed to approximately 290 million people in 2001). The point of this illustration is to show that those with a vested interest often use either raw numbers or percentages, depending upon which most benefits their argument. While a "$3 million dollar increase in sales" sounds impressive, it's nothing special if the company had $1 billion in sales. Similarly, a "300 percent increase in sales" sounds impressive, until you learn that the company's total sales for the previous year were under $100,000, and that "300 percent increase" was due to the company landing one new account.

Numbers — even if derived from accurate measurements — are constructs. The fundamental question is this: are these constructs accurate representations of reality, or are they merely presented to promote a specific point of view?

For further reading

The following are three recommended books that speak directly to math and statistics as they relate to both business and life in general:

Innumeracy: Mathematical Illiteracy and Its Consequences, by John Allen Paulos. Hill and Wang (a division of Farrar, Straus and Giroux), 2001. ISBN: 0-8090-5840-5.

Misused Statistics: Straight Talk for Twisted Numbers, by A.J. Jaffe and Herbert F. Spirer. Marcel Dekker Press, 1999. ISBN: 0824702115.

Tainted Truth: The Manipulation of Fact in America, by Cynthia Crossen. A Touchstone Book (a division of Simon & Schuster), 1994. ISBN: 0-671-79285-7.

Chapter Twelve

Multi-Media Mania
Don't be afraid of television and radio reporting

Robert Reed

In this era of non-stop information, the print-based press still has a tremendous advantage because its primary focus is to cover, and uncover, news — not just act as a distributor of content. Therefore, the best print reporters and editors are often tapped by other media outlets, especially radio and television, because they are the strongest sources for original reporting, new information and thoughtful analysis.

This is especially true for business reporting, where it's essential to explain events and their consequences. The trick for print journalists is making the leap from telling what you know in hundreds, even thousands, of words on the printed page to a much broader listening or viewing audience in a distilled yet informative manner.

Why do it?

Print journalists who embrace, rather than fight, this trend will find it raises their profile in the community. It also can further relationships with sources and help to make new contacts. Why? Frankly, supplementing your print work with a few well-placed radio and TV interviews and appearances can help send a significant message: You're a force to be reckoned with. Your words and ideas are carried beyond the business readers to a much wider audience, and that means greater exposure for you, your sources and your employer.

And for the more career-minded, it's also a good way for the boss to notice you. On the other hand, if you consistently refuse to tackle multi-media assignments, that's also a good way to get noticed by the boss — in an unfavorable light. Remember, your editors' bosses are seeing other reporters from competing papers or news organizations on air and they'll want to know why their celebrated staff isn't doing the same.

What to say, how to say it

Broadcast interviews are not known for being nuanced. And business reporting is often nuanced to a fault. While newspaper and magazines are made for that type of reporting, broadcasting is another beast. In many ways, being "on-air" will force print journalists to make their points quickly and draw conclusions. This is not something print reporters are always comfortable doing. However, with a little forethought it can be managed so that you won't be embarrassed and your credibility will remain intact.

Know the type of show you will be on. What's the broadcast format? News? Talk? Is it local? Syndicated? Being interviewed on National Public Radio is different than being quizzed by your local shock jock. Just remember, there are all sorts of radio and TV formats out there. Also, as a guest, will you be touted as an "expert" or an "informed observer"? Know the difference. For instance, some shows take phone calls from people who may want personal finance advice, and if that's not your expertise it can end up being a very long broadcast for you and everyone else involved. Also, it pays to do some fast research on the show that's calling you. Before agreeing, for example, find out if the host has a strict political or other agenda. (This is NOT to say you should stay away from formats that have pronounced views or are controversial. Just understand what you're getting into before you agree to participate.)

Understand your story. You may be called to report on a story you did a while back. Go back and read it. A little refresher course can keep the babbling to a minimum.

Be yourself—to a point. The best interviews occur when there's a real conversation happening between the host and guest, rather than a stilted Q-and-A session. It takes a confident host and guest to make this dynamic work. That said, this is not just your average chat. You're there to discuss a story, or something happening on the beat,

Performing vs. talking

Print journalists don't like to admit this but it takes skill to read a teleprompter naturally. It's true that the news readers who do this are performing, but that's what they're supposed to do — read and project a personality that connects with viewers. Our advice to those print journalists doing TV: Unless you are schooled and skilled in reading the prompter, just say "no"! Instead, go for the interview.

so don't get carried away by talking about yourself and the process of getting the story. Don't get detoured with too many unimportant asides. Stay focused. If you can, ask the show's producer, who calls to line up your appearance, for a little guidance on the topic to be discussed. Bear in mind that there are all types of producers. Some really run the show while others won't have a clue about what's going to happen. Even so, it doesn't hurt to ask.

Talking numbers: When someone reads a newspaper or magazine, she can go back and reread or check on a fact or figure that's unclear or confusing. Not so with broadcast. So try and keep remarks as simple (but informative) as you can. You don't have to recite every source, number or factoid that makes a story or beat coverage. Often one, or two, well-placed comparative numbers can make a compelling point. For example: "The company's profits were down 70 percent from the same time last year. But it still made $10 million." Or "Social Security checks are going up 2.5 percent. That's an average of $25 a week."

What's heard vs. what's said. Sometimes, what people hear isn't what is actually being said. You can't avoid that disconnect, but an attempt should be made to limit such confusion. For example, when talking about the problems of a bank during a broadcast interview, some people may freak and think the bank is going bust. If it isn't, it helps to throw in a line noting the institution is still solid and deposits are insured by the federal government. Just remember that not every one tuning in is a business expert, so you have to explain situations, terms and facts in a way that's clear to even the casual viewer or listener. A good interviewer should help you do this, but that's not always the case.

Opinion makers. What you say will be magnified by the electronic media, so it's wise to keep personal opinions about leaders, situations and companies to a minimum — even if the host eggs you on.

Don't get trapped into saying a company is on the brink of disaster if it's just run into a serious situation that has to be fixed. That said, be secure enough to honestly analyze a situation or circumstance. This is why you're on the air! For example, if your experience and reporting tell you that Company X is headed for trouble, then it's fair to draw that conclusion. Remember, you're being quizzed because of your expertise, so make the most of it.

Pot of gold?

To my knowledge, there's no huge payday out there for most print journalists who make the multi-media leap. Enlightened employers give incentives or bonuses to those reporters who make the effort to do broadcast work and carry the print publication's banner. Sometimes, there is a token payment from the broadcast outlets for guests on panel shows or public affairs programs. There's usually no money for appearing on news programs as a source (that's as it should be). Right now, my opinion is that this work should be viewed almost as a public service. You are telling a wider audience something worthwhile and important. That may not get you a down payment on a new house or sports car, but it's worth a great deal to improving public discourse.

Company plan

We've outlined some of the reasons why an individual journalist would want to go multi-media, especially in radio and TV. Now here's why a print-based news organization should seek to build partnerships and relationships with radio and TV news outlets.

Think strategically. There are many ways a newspaper can get into the electronic news game. In some markets, media companies already own the local newspaper and a radio or TV station, perhaps even a cable news outlet. In such cases, top management usually "persuades" the print reporters to cooperate with the broadcast side of the company either by appearing on air or providing information that can be scripted and then crafted into a business news segment.

There are other ways, too. Business editors can enter into formal partnerships with radio or TV stations and do daily news reports, or regular market analysis and updates. Often these are done remote from the newspaper's newsroom, which cuts down on time-consuming commutes between the newspaper's office and broadcast studio.

(Please note: Even a broadcast report that's only a couple of minutes long is time-consuming. It may require some original reporting, updating or just shuttling to a studio. So anything that can ease those burdens for deadline-weary journalists is a plus.)

In other situations, broadcast stations will have a more informal "consulting" relationship with the business news staff, opting to use print experts on big business news or breaking news. No matter what approach, a good print-broadcast deal is one that works for both the newspaper and the station.

Build a brand. One major motivation for entering into a broadcast deal is to build "brand awareness" of a newspaper's business coverage. In formal agreements with TV stations, where the print staff is a regular contributor, the newspaper publisher should insist on getting "on-screen" signage or billing of the newspaper's logo and name. In a TV deal, publishers should also press for the use of "on-screen" identification of its reporters along with the newspaper's

What type of stories get on air?

There are certain types of stories that translate well on TV and radio. Here are some ideas:

Things we all do. Everybody eats, travels and shops. As a result, stories that broadcast news directors often seek for their "general" audience have to do with retail, airlines and food companies.

Name brands. We all have a connection with well-known name brands. McDonald's, Coca-Cola, Disney, American Airlines and Microsoft are all examples. Stories that tell something about their relationships with the buying public get picked up. The same goes for well-known local brands like the regional store chain or the town's biggest employer.

Corporate corruption. Everyone loves a good scandal. Unfortunately, we've had no shortage of those in the business world lately. Lawsuits, indictments, government crackdowns are always in demand. The trick is distilling these complicated matters into short on-air bites.

Your workplace. Boss gets on your nerves? Want to work more from home? Trying to get a raise? We spend a lot of time in the workplace and stories on new workplace trends are in demand.

Your money. I'm not a big fan of personal finance advice over the air. The best you can hope for is some honest guidance and referrals to the proper sources. Nevertheless, this is an area that broadcast stations like to highlight.

name. Many times TV stations identify sources only as "business experts" and forget to use their professional affiliation or identification. The point is to showcase the newspaper's business coverage and to project that image into the far reaches of the community — often to people who may not read the business section. As for radio deals — insist on the proper on-air mentions. Also, remember this is a two-way deal, so it is highly likely that your broadcast partners will negotiate with the newspaper to provide regular promotional mentions touting the stations' business reports and the partnership.

Own the story. The news cycle for broadcast is different than print. Use that to your advantage! Did your staff get beat on a big story? Did a story break at a bad time during the newspaper's cycle — like first thing Monday morning or over the weekend? It happens. In addition to scrambling like hell to regain the competitive edge, business news staffs can get back fast into the game and in the flow of the developing story by tapping into their electronic media outlets and partnerships. Bear in mind, local TV and radio assignment editors don't care if your newspaper got beat on the story; they'll want your people to comment on it anyway. Do it. Use those radio and TV appearances as a way to advance the story that's breaking or to offer some fresh perspective on it. We're not suggesting that newspaper people scoop themselves on-air by revealing to the world what the "second-day lead" on the breaking story will be in tomorrow's paper. But some well placed interviews and reports can help your newspaper keep its competitive edge.

Money or barter? There may come a day when broadcast outlets will pay big bucks to features newspaper staffers on air, but that time has not arrived. In most cases, these deals are viewed by business people as pure marketing, or barter, agreements between the two news organizations. The broadcast outlets provide the electronic delivery system and the newspapers pony up the content. Such arrangements can get complicated when unions are involved, however. To get around any problems, companies will have to seek a waiver from the unions to make these cross-platform deals a reality. Others opt to fight the unions by arguing that these deals are marketing-based, not editorial-based, and therefore exempt from any labor agreements or contracts. Unions are starting to push back on these arrangements, so management needs to be aware of that reaction.

How I became a talking dog

It's harder than it looks.

Like many print journalists, I had a smug attitude about broadcast news. Print was where REAL news was covered, not TV or radio. In Texas, where I worked for the Dallas Times Herald (now defunct), print reporters referred to broadcast journalists as "talking dogs."

Ask a fellow reporter who was at a press conference and the reply would go something like this: "The News, AP, and some talking dogs..."

My attitude changed once I started doing regular television and radio reports and realized how much work goes into every segment and the skill set that's needed to communicate with viewers and listeners. I've been doing TV and radio (while still working in print) for over 10 years and continue to marvel at what it takes to be a good broadcast journalist.

As an editor at the regional business publication Crain's Chicago Business, I was among a trio of Crain's journalists picked to anchor business news segments on WMAQ-TV, Chicago's NBC affiliate. This arrangement was new to Crain's and the station. No one knew how, or if, it would work. I also oversaw the daily editorial management of the broadcast experiment.

Crain's viewed the deal as a way to build its franchise as a provider of local business news. WMAQ-TV sought to leverage off the Crain's name and offer viewers something its competitors didn't. There was also speculation that business news would attract upscale viewers, predominately males, and that local banks, financial service firms and other upscale corporate advertisers would sponsor the reports.

The three-to-four minute segments (a long span in a TV show with about 24 minutes of content) were beamed from the Crain's newsroom. Sounds simple, but retrofitting an older building, where Crain's worked from, with a satellite dish, proper lighting, a computer that was compatible with the station's editorial system, and a camera with a teleprompter was not an easy chore and took many weeks.

TV stations are pretty frugal (OK, cheap). The equipment used outside the main station is often comprised of cast-offs. The WMAQ-TV stuff at Crain's was so old the TV engineers would laugh when they came by to fix or maintain it — which was often.

Then there were the broadcast unions. Until the station worked out a deal with its unions, station employees traveled across downtown

Chicago to the Crain's office to flick on one light switch. They would also sit next to the Crain's "anchor" and turn the knob that controlled the pace of the teleprompter. (After getting union clearance, Crain's "anchors" were allowed to turn on the equipment and work the teleprompter dial.)

The segments were supposed to be based on stories that appeared in the weekly Crain's. However, one learned fast that a great story for a business section or periodical didn't always cut it with TV producers. They tended to look for business stories that appealed to consumers and a wider audience. As a result, consumer products, airlines, travel, housing and other broad topics made air. Lay-offs were always big news.

I was lucky to work with an experienced TV producer who liked business news. Norb Tatro had been at NBC (local and network) for years. He'd package the segments, conjuring up graphics, pulling file footage and fighting to get crews to go out and shoot fresh video when it applied (unless you have a strike or plane crash, business news is pretty hard to illustrate on TV). I learned that without a good producer you're cooked.

Crain's reporters wrote for themselves, which required learning how to write in broadcast style — a much more direct, conversational style than print.

It's fair to say the first few weeks of broadcasts were train wrecks. The "anchors" were inexperienced and nervous. It showed. The lights were hot, the print on the teleprompter would suddenly go black and there were, after all, thousands of people watching the show. Let the flop sweat flow....

But the station and Crain's management remained committed to the deal and eventually we got more comfortable and the segments got better. They were even good sometimes!

It was a lot of work. Some days it required staying late until show time. Other times, it pulled people off print deadlines. There was in-house grumbling, too. Since the camera was set up in the midst of the newsroom, the work of nearby reporters was interrupted by the "lights, camera and action" aspect of it all.

After a nearly three-year run, the Crain's segment was cancelled when new management took over the station. The segment was moved over to the Fox owned-and-operated station (WFLD-TV) and aired there for nearly two years (I was solo anchor) before it ended.

A few years later, Crain's returned to the air by appearing weekly on Chicago Tonight, a news and information show on Chicago's PBS affiliate, WTTW. In this capacity, the anchor would interview a Crain's on-air editor or reporter — a tactic that allows him or her to focus more on content than a teleprompter.

All in all, some important lessons were learned.

■ TV people are smart. The good ones know their jobs and their medium. Once trust is established, listen to them and follow their lead. Not once has a TV producer I've worked with interfered with the content of a business story. But they have worked with me to find ways of telling the stories better.

■ Become part of the show. Try to have some fun with the stories. You don't have to be a stand-up comedian. But crack a smile, interact with the main anchors and don't take yourself, or your story, so seriously that you encourage viewers to turn the dial.

■ Don't quit your day job. Business news is not mainstream and never will be. Yes, CNBC has carved out a place. But on local newscasts, it's a segment—like sports—that attracts a certain type of viewer.

Finally, should you get the opportunity to do TV, go for it. After all, every dog—whether it talks or not — should have its day.

Index